Hamburgers, Cocktails & Rock n' Roll

The Story of the Palm Suite Restaurant

By David E. Williams

Copyright © 2023 by David E. Williams

All rights reserved. No part of this book may be reproduced or used in any manner without written permission of the copyright owner except for the use of quotations in a book review.

ISBNs
Paperback: 978-1-80541-204-5
Hardcover: 978-1-80541-206-9
eBook: 978-1-80541-205-2

Dedication

There are two people I wish to dedicate this book to, and of course the first is my mother and business partner, the lovely owner you know as Edna, who worked tirelessly to achieve her dream of owning a successful restaurant.

Your love and passion for cooking never ends. Thank you for so many successful recipes and all those desserts you still cooked until the end. I am so proud to have been part of it.

The second person who helped us so much to open the Palm Suite and who, over the years, became somebody I always considered to be my best friend, is John Ellner, who owned Joanna's in Crystal Palace. He is no longer with us today but he is forever in my thoughts.

Introduction

This book is about how the Palm Suite Restaurant started back in 1981. We became famous for our great hamburgers, so you won't find out how to cook Michelin-star food in this book. We spent 34 years cooking good, honest food using quality ingredients and we now reveal some of our very popular early recipes.

I always believed dining out should be an overall enjoyable experience. The average time we spend in a restaurant is about 2 hours, but we only spend about 20 minutes of that eating, so atmosphere and ambience are important. The Palm Suite was full of film memorabilia, signed pictures, subdued lighting, cocktails and definitely some rock and roll!

This all helps, but the best thing about the Palm Suite was the millions of customers who joined in our fun over the 34 years. So many of you became such good regulars.

Thank you all so much; you made it all worthwhile.

Contents

Part 1: The history of Palm Suite Restaurant and the Pinewood Studios Connection

Chapter 1 - 34 years as a Restaurateur.. 1
Chapter 2 - Our First Night... 8
Chapter 3 - Promotion & Advertising (but make it fun!)................................ 11
Chapter 4 - Our First Christmas Eve, 1981.. 17
Chapter 5 - Our First Pinewood Studios Dinner... 20
Chapter 6 - Star-spotting at the Palm Suite.. 29
Chapter 7 - Not a Typical Monday Night in the Restaurant......................... 43
Chapter 8 - I Met John Malkovich.. 45
Chapter 9 - The Avengers... 47
Chapter 10 - For Your Eyes Only and the James Bond Film Crew............ 50
Chapter 11 - No Sinking Feeling About These Movies.................................. 60
Chapter 12 - Holy Hollywood, Batman's Being Filmed at Pinewood!..... 64
Chapter 13 - Saturday Night's Alright For Fighting....................................... 67
Chapter 14 - The Naked Diner (no pictures included).................................. 68
Chapter 15 - The Iver Heath Locals... 70
Chapter 16 - My Role as a Restaurateur.. 74
Chapter 17 - Palm Suite Butchers.. 77

Part 2: Food & drink

Hamburgers.. 79
Homemade stocks 106
Bowls and small plates 114
Large plates... 141
Cocktails at the Palm Suite.. 202
Palm Sweets and Desserts... 232

Part 3: All good things come to an end

Rock n' Roll at the Palms.. 250
The Palm Court: Restaurant.. 258
Back to one Palm 263
Acknowledgements and Special Thanks... 282
Index 285

Restaurant front, 1981

Restaurant front, 2015

Chapter 1 — 34 years as a Restaurateur

My 34 years as a restaurateur started on 15th June, 1981. It took me the next 6 months to pronounce this French word correctly, which was my grand new job title. It took me years to remember how to spell it, but I now hope it's made me qualified to write this book.

I was previously in the printing business, which did not require any social skills. This certainly suited me as I would often feel nervous about meeting new people. If I'd had to be interviewed for this position of restaurateur, I would have gone hungry talking about food I knew absolutely nothing about.

It was by complete chance that I came into the restaurant business, even though my mother, Edna, always wanted to own one. It was through the meeting with a new pub landlord called John Ellner, who, it turned out, was also a printer, and we had worked at the same printing factory in South London, Crystal Palace. We never met there but we exchanged a few stories and became friends. His pub, called the 'Robin Hood' in Maidenhead, became one of the first gastro-type pubs. It didn't take long, with his fun-loving approach and serving great food, until the pub was a great success.

John didn't find working for the brewery very rewarding and so he headed back to his hometown of Crystal Palace, opening a restaurant called 'Joanna's'. This became an instant success and customers would form a queue outside just to get into the bar, to then wait for a table! Service was quick on a simple menu, including hamburgers, so diners were in and out quickly, usually having downed a couple of strong cocktails on the way. John invited us all to the restaurant, which made my mother more determined to open her own. When John offered his help, there was no stopping her. I also started to become more interested, and my second wife, Julie, decided to join in (not that she knew much about restaurants).

We started to look around for suitable premises, which was not easy in those days, as licensed restaurants and pubs rarely came onto the open market. Pubs would be full even at lunchtime when nobody worried about having a drink. What a wonderful fun-loving wobbly world we lived in then; of course, not wishing to glamorise drinking, but it could be a very profitable business if you got it right. On with the hunt, and I found an empty shop in Marlow. Not wishing to wait to view it with the agent, I jumped over the back fence of a small garden, only to be confronted by two Irish Wolfhounds leaping up at me. One had my arm in its jaws and the other was barking before the owner then appeared and called them off. I apologised and left with holes in my new leather jacket. I never went back, but it did turn into a wine bar for somebody.

My mother had found a place in Beaconsfield but it fell through; not quite right. Then we came across a new build in a place called Iver Heath. It had four shops with separate flats upstairs on a housing estate. Not the perfect location, in fact, most friends thought it was terrible and would never work; no passing trade so no one would find it. But it did have something going for it - no premium to get in and it was near Pinewood Studios. "How's that going to help?" was a typical remark, not that we or our friends knew much about Pinewood Studios.

After a lot of thought and debate, we decided to go for it and we soon signed the lease for 25 years, unheard of today, so we had to try and make it work. We chose the end unit that could be seen from the road that ran through Iver Heath, linking the M40 with the M4. There were traffic jams every day so the restaurant could get noticed. Later, I came up with the idea to get flyers printed, on reasons to visit the restaurant rather than sit in the traffic. This obviously was the right job for our good-looking waitresses, who, I have to say, certainly boosted trade.

Now it was time to roll up our sleeves and start turning this bare unit into a restaurant. So, with the help of some local builders, we got going, building walls, plastering and fixing toilets. Next, catering equipment, and none of us knew anything about what we should buy.

We gave our friend John a call who went round London buying second-hand catering equipment. He saved us a fortune and the best bit of kit was the charcoal grill, which we used for 25 years. To light it, you would turn the gas on, throw a match in the top and stand back. Crazy really, but it always lit and never killed any of our chefs, and there were certainly a few I could have happily done that to over the years.

The restaurant was starting to take shape - John found a shop that had 50 second-hand bentwood chairs and old 60's-type tables going cheap and had them delivered on a Saturday afternoon. We then spent Saturday evening cleaning them. A quick coat of varnish and then they were okay. It had that used popular look of any good busy restaurant.

Now that we had tables and chairs, we could start interviewing for staff. Back in 1981, you could advertise for barmen and waitresses and you could even state the age of the applicant. We, of course, never did any such thing, but our staff were employed for many good reasons and they all helped us enhance the progress. The kitchen equipment was being connected up and the cooking started, mainly new test dishes for our first menu.

Next to arrive was my custom-made cocktail bar. I was very proud of my design until the girls pointed out how high it was, so high you could only just about see Barbara's head (our first full-time waitress, admittedly not a tall girl). Out with the saws and we cut a couple of feet off the bottom. Barbara was an incredibly good waitress and looked and walked like Marilyn Monroe. If any the Pinewood film lads were getting saucy with her, it was mother to the rescue.

To Start:

1. HOMEMADE SOUP — 65p
   of the day
2. PRAWN COCKTAIL — 1.10
3. CUP OF CHILLI — 1.15
   Garnished with sour cream & served with corn chips
4. CORN ON THE COB — 90p
   served with melted butter & black pepper
5. DEEP FRIED CLAMS — 1.65
   Delicious & something not to miss
6. FRESHLY MADE QUICHE — 90p
   served hot or cold

To Follow:

Our 6oz. 100% ground beef hamburgers are chargrilled to order, served with french fries or jacket potato, and accompanied by one of our mouthwatering salads, — all included in the price!

7. BASIC BURGER — 2.25
   Straight from the chargrill
8. CHEESE BURGER — 2.50
   with melted cheese
9. WAISTLINE BURGER — 2.50
   served on rye crisp with cottage cheese & fresh fruits
10. CHILLI BURGER — 2.65
    smothered in chilli sauce
11. SUPER BURGER — 2.65
    served with delicious wine & mushroom sauce
12. 8oz SIRLOIN STEAK — 4.95
    cooked to your liking & served with french fries or jacket potato & a salad of your choice
13. MINUTE STEAK — 3.20
    served with french fries or jacket potato & a salad of your choice
14. GOURMET CHICKEN — 3.50
    ½ a roasted chicken served with or without our homemade wine & mushroom sauce & a salad of your choice
15. STEAK KEBABS IN OYSTER SAUCE — 4.50
    cubes of fresh steak, chargrilled with onions, peppers & our exotic oyster sauce, served with jacket potato & salad of your choice
16. FRESHLY MADE QUICHE — 2.50
    served with salad of your choice and french fries or jacket potato
17. CHILLI CON CARNE — 2.50
    A bowl of chilli topped with sour cream & garnished with corn chips, onion rings & sliced pitta bread
18. PALM SALAD — 3.50
    Exotic fresh fruits, crunchy coleslaw & cottage cheese, nuts and raisins

SALADS

a) MIXED SALAD
   Choice of dressing
b) WALDORF SALAD
   Apple, celery, walnuts & raisins in mayonnaise & served on bed of lettuce
c) FRESH CUCUMBER, MINT & ONION SALAD
d) CRUNCHY COLESLAW
e) AMERICAN SALAD
   Pineapple, carrots, peppers & raisins in a seafood dressing

SIDE ORDERS

DEEP FRIED ONION RINGS — 50p
FLASH FRIED MUSHROOMS — 50p
FRENCH FRIES — 40p
JACKET POTATO — 40p

Desserts:

All desserts served with whipped cream unless otherwise asked

19. HOT WAFFLE & MAPLE SYRUP — 1.00
20. COUNTRY APPLE PIE — 85p
    hot or cold
21. BLACK CHERRY BRANDY CHEESECAKE — 85p
22. ICE CREAM FUDGE SUNDAE — 1.00
23. FRESHLY MADE BAKEWELL TART — 85p
    Splendidly almondy
24. COFFEE — 35p

All prices inclusive of V.A.T.

Our very first menu, June 15th 1981 (price sticker added in September and the dish became even more popular!)

Mother was very fond of Barbara, our sweet and innocent waitress, who was having an affair with one of my married mates.

Well, that's another story, so back to opening this restaurant. The bar went in, painted in dark mahogany varnish and the top had a marbled effect Formica, very popular in the 60s and it should have stayed there. This was my cocktail bar and I was very proud of it. I had made special speed rails for the making of cocktails and a lit-up back bar showing off all the different coloured liqueurs. Cocktails in the 80s were just taking off as a drink that was drunk by anybody, not by the elite rich in the 1920s. The cocktail drinks turned out to be a massive success for the restaurant.

Just in case you thought I had this amazing talent for setting up bars, it was again my best mate John who helped me do all the drinks' orders and arrange the bar. He taught me how to make cocktails in his fabulous restaurant Joanna's in Crystal Palace. John helped many people set up bars and restaurants over the years but he always told me I was his success story. That was better than winning a Michelin Star, not that they gave hamburger joints any awards in those days (although the Buckinghamshire Advertiser did vote us the best cocktail bar in the county, which certainly boosted business).

The restaurant was now starting to take shape, food was coming in and fridges were being filled ready for the big night. We still hadn't named the restaurant, so we decided to have a big family Sunday lunch and try to come up with a name. I wanted the restaurant to have a fun summer beach feel to it. We all loved the name 'The Coconut Grove', an Antony Worrall Thompson restaurant in London. It was a great restaurant and always packed. Someone suggested 'Palm Trees', 'Beach Palms', even 'Windy Palms' - I was not sure it would sound right for Iver Heath. My father's suggestion of 'Iver Big One' got thrown out immediately.

Then someone said, 'The Palm Suite', and from then on, we have all taken credit for naming The Palm Suite Restaurant. By this time, my father had started to get used to the fact that his wife was going to open a restaurant, which he was originally dead against. So much so, that they nearly split up over it, but they didn't and, in fact, Mother got him doing front of house on a Saturday night. Meeting and greeting customers, hanging coats up and showing them to tables was not really his scene. My father knew a lot about running a business and was a good company accountant, so he then offered to set up and do the books. This was the perfect role for him and he guided us financially for many years.

We had been setting up now for over two months and our three-month rent-free period was running out. So we asked John if he could come down from London and do a checklist meeting with us to make sure we were ready to go. On his arrival, around 1.00 pm, he immediately suggested the pub around the corner, The Stag & Hounds, a rather small pub with three bars that was very popular.

My mother Edna (far left) and myself (far right with my sister Susan) with our first friendly team

This film was released in January 18th, 1967 and was one of our first film posters in 1981 and was shot on location in Venice

"Have to check out all the local competition," he would tell us. In he walked and ordered a round of drinks, introducing us to the landlord and locals as the mad lot that was opening the restaurant around the corner. They also found this amusing, saying it would never work as they had a Bernie Inn down the road. The pub was also full of the construction guys from Pinewood Studios who seemed to be enjoying a bevy or two. This got me thinking more about the Studios - where do the film technical guys go for lunch and how do we get them to the Palm Suite Restaurant?

Our checklist was not going well by this time and the pub was shutting at 2.30pm, so we settled down to the meeting. John started to find lots of things we had missed, so we started job lists. Then he found the big clanger, very big, as we had not applied for a drinks licence. We got on the phone to the council to apply for one and discovered that being a new licence, this was dealt with by the courts. So we got a date very quickly, which had to be attended by my mother and Julie to be the licensees. I was still working in the printing business during the day, just helping here and there.

Everything was now in place, so we were just waiting for the licence. The big day arrived, which turned out more nerve-racking than they thought as neither had been to a court before. This was not a bad thing, as they did not easily grant a licence to anyone with a criminal record. They had to attend Beaconsfield Magistrate's Court to apply for the licence and they were not keen on granting a new drinks licence in this residential area, as there was a local pub and an off-licence. Everyone is extremely serious in courts and when the Magistrate looked over his glasses, they felt like they were going to be sent to the gallows. Mother and Julie had to pull out all their best answers to the questions, then just smiled sweetly. It was granted and they thanked everyone including the clerks. It was not a straightforward licence as we could not sell alcohol unless you were eating. Then we had to close after 2.30 pm, open at 6.00 pm and no more drinks after 10.30 pm Monday to Thursday, or 11.00 pm Friday and Saturday. Then on top of all that, no Sundays! This, of course, seems very strange now, as there are very few restrictions on when you can buy a drink.

Restaurant interior, 1980s

Sandy and Edna living up to our motto: "The Palm Suite's a fun restaurant, but we are not a joke"

One of our first old film posters - in French!

Chapter 2 — Our First Night

We had been building up to this moment it seemed like forever, and when it finally arrived, we were petrified. I took the day off work at the printing factory to help set everything up. Mother was in the kitchen helping the chefs, and Julie was out the front setting up the restaurant with Barbara. In fact, Barbara was mopping the floor, not her favourite job but something she religiously did every morning. I was helping our full-time barman Sandy set up the bar, a man who I never thought at the time wanted to really be in catering. His parents were both in the police force and they had other ambitions for him. His father was famous for catching a famous nasty criminal. Anyway, he never joined the police force. He left us the following week but came back three days later and stayed for six and a half years.

John arrived at lunchtime to help us set up and check things over. We put him up in a local bed & breakfast which I don't think he was too impressed with. We worked hard into the afternoon and the restaurant was ready to go. The first night, we had just invited friends as a warm-up, which is now called a soft launch, so an easy seat and greet with food and the first cocktails on the house. John asked me for a gin and tonic, so I opened the ice machine door and it was empty - "no ice, John". He told me to nip down to the Holiday Inn and ask if I could have some. This turned out to be a great idea as they had ice machines on every floor; loads of ice. I had of course asked the receptionist and bribed her with a free meal and cocktails. This was a great investment because our first ice machine was always breaking down.

We now had ice and we were ready to rock and roll, friends were arriving and the cocktails were flowing. We finally got everyone seated for food and Barbara and her waitress team zoomed around to take orders. Our menu was small - six easy starters, hamburgers and a few other dishes. I don't think everyone got the right meals, but nobody seemed to mind. It's amazing how jolly everyone was after a couple of cocktails and the wine was flowing. Now, this was the biggest test for the waitresses - clearing the dinner plates. My mother had given the girls some silver service training and was very keen to see them carry the plates properly. This did not go to plan, as they tried to balance them on one arm and walk to the wash up area, but it seemed like more was going to the bin. We soon scrapped the silver service training that night.

The dancing started and the music went up and we were bending the licence laws on the first night. This was certainly a plus for starting a restaurant tucked out of the way. Our party came to an end and a good time was had by all.

The next night was for all tradesmen and their bosses who had worked and helped us put the restaurant together, our way of saying thank you. The evening went well and John added a few extra people who were just walking past or looking to see what we were up to. John was not keen to stay in the bed & breakfast so he left us now to our own devices.

The next night was a big come down as we only had five in all evening. Our first paying customers were a local couple who decided to tell us where we were going wrong, a common thing that happens to restaurateurs on quiet nights. Unfortunately, we were going to get loads of these over the next six months.

The following three were from the Stag & Hounds, including the landlord, who liked a good drink and loved the cocktails. He turned into our first good diner spending loads of time in the Palm Suite, possibly too much time as he was given his marching orders from the brewery. He disappeared, proving you can't run a pub from the cocktail bar next door.

Our original palm tree logo in 1981

From left to right: John Ellner, my father Cyril and myself on opening night by the bar

A visit to John's restaurant in Crystal Palace, 'Joanna's', 1981 (the good old days when you could park outside).

Chapter 3 — Promotion & Advertising (but make it fun!)

When we first opened, we very soon became aware we needed as much of this as we could get. None of us had any experience in this field, with no budget to promote a new restaurant business hidden away on a housing estate. We decided we had to invest in some leaflets with menu information, our palm tree logo and a map showing how to find us. Maps can be quite boring, and by chance, Sandy had a friend who was an illustrator and cartoonist, who drew us an amusing map. He took his fee in food and drink for several evenings. We did lots of payments of this nature over the years, which is legal and certainly helped the cash flow.

We did not have any money to have the leaflets delivered, so, in our breaks, or if the session was looking quiet, l would leave the staff and start distributing them anywhere that might drum up trade, on people's cars in high streets, pub car parks (best done at night-time), factories and offices. The local cinema car parks always brought in a few late-night diners. Early weeknights, I could be out for hours. We had no mobile phones so if the restaurant got busy, they would send the washer-up out to get me.

The restaurant could be seen from the busy road after I cut down all the bushes that hid us. I had some more leaflets made up, always with the map on, and on the other side it said, "Why sit in a jam when you can sit beneath a palm tree sipping a cocktail?" Then I sent the waitresses out at the 5 pm traffic jam alongside the restaurant handing them to drivers. It worked probably because I and the barman weren't handing them out.

One of the best places to promote us was the hairdressers, as this gave them something new to talk about other than the usual holidays, and they always had menus at hand. A hairdresser opened in our parade of four shops and the owner was a young, trendy guy who loved our cocktails. This was perfect as we could use him, his staff and customers to test out our cocktails, so, many a lunchtime, I was running cocktails into the salon. This was great fun and the more they drank the more they promoted us. I am not too sure whether I would want my haircut on one of these tasting sessions with all the laughter, giggling and mucking around that was going on, but they said their haircuts got better and the customers loved it.

Local newspaper advertising could be very good exposure but expensive, so the adverts had to be good and eye-catching. Sandy, my full-time barman, had a great dry sense of humour, the perfect person to help me do the advertising. Many an afternoon we would sit down working on different adverts and he would have me in stitches of laughter at his funny ideas, using lots of his quotes.

This caused quite a stir in Iver Heath, drawing sharks around the Crooked Billet was just a joke!

One of the best adverts was when one of us got on the idea to do a pirate's map, showing Palm Suite on an island. We wanted it so that people could find us, so we put in local landmarks and roads with a palm tree at the restaurant. The island showed the Crooked Billet pub, which was a very successful Bernie Inn, a chain of steak restaurants. We drew sharks around it with a 'beware' sign which made us laugh, but the manager at the time did not see the funny side. When the paper came out that Friday morning, he came to see us with his copy telling us we had to remove the sharks and he would be writing to his head office. He left in a bit of a rage, throwing the newspaper across the restaurant. We never did remove the sharks and repeated the advert in all the local newspapers and trade went up. I also noticed more cars in his car park, so maybe his trade went up too as he didn't complain again.

In the 80s, car stickers were very popular, so we thought we would knock one up. As the restaurant was hard to find, we came up with the idea of it saying, "I've Found The Palm Suite Restaurant at Iver Heath." That was it and of course we all put them on our cars and gave hundreds away to our customers. Just as well we had a friendly regular who printed them for us and it was easy to exchange services. It was a great way to pay someone in food and drink. We all started to see the car stickers on our journeys and fellow drivers would wave to each other. I was often asked where the restaurant was in Iver Heath when I parked up. It was easy for me, as I always had map leaflets in the car to hand out. Then a reporter, who was on holiday in Bahrain, 3,000 miles from Iver Heath, spotted one of our car stickers on an American limousine. He took a photo of it with a local Arab. On his return, the Slough Observer printed the picture with a story. That was good free publicity.

No satnavs in 1981, so we loved map advertising

In the eighties and nineties, every town had a local newspaper. Iver Heath was too small, but as Uxbridge was one side of Iver Heath and Slough was the other side, we had good choice. If you booked a run of six adverts, they would offer you a free write-up. The norm was the reporter with a friend would come along and have a free meal. It didn't take me long to realise the more you gave, the larger and better the write-up would be. A three-course meal with cocktails, wine and liqueurs would sometimes get you a double-page write-up, as well as very drunk reporters. I would try and get them to write a constructive review without sounding like we were best friends (although maybe I was after that amount of free drink!).

I used to love doing theme nights such as July 4th American Independence Day, with a three-course American meal and American wines. We would dress up in American clothes, where I was an American Naval officer one year. We did a Wild West Night dressing up as cowboys and Indians, and I got one of our regular customers to bring the horse along and give the local kids free rides. Bonkers really, as we had no insurance for such an event.

Halloween was quite a good one, but the real big event in the 80s was Beaujolais Nouveau in November. This was a very popular lunch and dinner party and all the Pinewood film lads used to enjoy the event. If you've never heard of Beaujolais Nouveau, it is the first wine of the current year, bottled very quickly and representing the quality of that year's vintage. It was a very young and fruity wine, with most years tasting just about okay. It also gave you a bad hangover, but that perhaps was more to do with the amount you drank.

Myself (right) and our part-time barman on Wild West Night - one of the few nights I allowed the young lads to drink out of the bottles

I always liked to theme the restaurant with French flags and bunting; play some French music and cook some French specials, such as snails, frogs legs, Beef Bourguignon and Chicken Kiev. It was good, but I still wanted to make it more entertaining. I suddenly had a great idea to have Can-can dancers. I mentioned this idea to the waitresses and it turned out I was employing trained dancers. This could not be better as they could practice the famous dance after a waitress shift. As we got closer to the event, I advertised the Beaujolais Nouveau evening, featuring Fifi and Chloe, the famous Can-can dancers from the Moulin Rouge. This created a lot of interest and the bookings started rolled in.

The evening came and we started the show at about 8.30 pm. Dining with us that evening was a lot of regulars, and with one of our parties from Pinewood was the famous film director, Ken Russell. This was great for our dancers as they had planned to involve some diners in teaching them the Can-can dance. This was great fun, and was a good laugh with the first chaps, with rolled up trousers and frilly Can-can skirts on, trying the dancing kicks with the dancers. The girls then asked Ken Russell and he was all for joining in. On with the skirt and up went his legs with the high Can-can kicks. What a good sport he was! Lots of customers took photos of him and he received a big round of applause when he finished.

Ken Russell taking time off from filming Lady Chatterley, in 1993; he also cast him- self into the series as Sir Michael Reid.

Ken enjoyed the odd glass of wine and was always ready to join in the fun!

If you are starting a restaurant, I can definitely recommend you do theme nights. Unfortunately, the popularity of Beaujolais Nouveau died a death, which is very disappointing for us restaurateurs, but there are plenty of others and Elvis nights are always very popular.

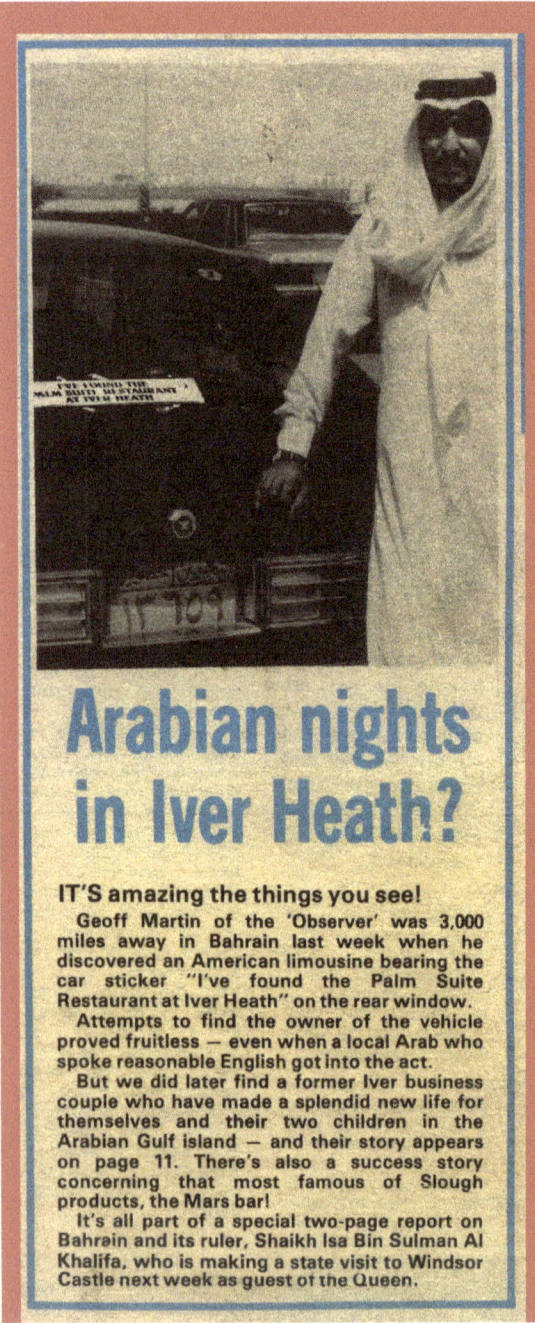

Left photo: There is nothing like free advertising! This was printed in one of our local newspapers.

Below photo: Advertising cocktails was always another good way to get extra diners.

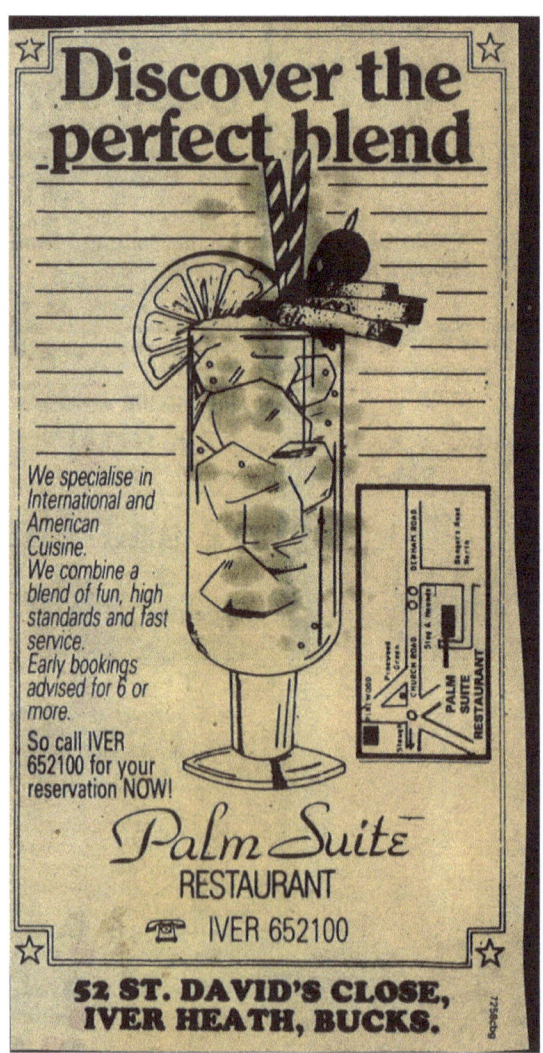

Chapter 4 — Our First Christmas Eve, 1981

I employed a new barman called Simon who happened to live near me in Marlow. I was forever having to bring him in due to his unreliable car, but I am sure it was the way he use to drive it - far too fast, crashing the gears... I don't know how he ever passed his test. He frightened the life out of me one night driving me in. Never again!

Anyway, it was a snowy Christmas Eve and he phoned me up for a lift in as his old car was not very good on the snow and he needed new front tyres. I agreed but told him to drive down to my house at 5.30 pm and not to be late, as he normally was.

At 5.30 pm, I went outside to wait for Simon, noticing my neighbour was also outside with his dog running around in the snow. He came over to chat to me, telling me that him and his wife were just off out with the dog to see friends. I did suggest he put his dog in the car as my barman, the mad driver, would be coming down the road hopefully soon. He put the dog in the car just as I saw Simon's car coming down the long road. Our part of the road had not been de-iced, as Simon found out as he veered sideways heading towards us and my neighbour's car. We both ran as he crashed into his brand new car. It was quite a bang and I rushed over to see if Simon was okay. My neighbour was more interested in his dog but he couldn't get the back door open. The dog, a big South African Ridgeback, was fine and jumped over the back seat and out. Simon was also fine until my neighbour wanted to hit him. He didn't, but instead told him he was an idiot. "It's only a car and will be repaired, and nobody was hurt, man or beast."

This was not a good start to our first Christmas Eve at the restaurant and we were running late. My neighbour's wife then came out and went mad, as they then had to go to their dinner party in her small sports car with the dog in the middle. The three of them looked very funny squeezed in; she was a very grumpy wife but the husband looked rather smug, as he had now got out of doing the driving. I rushed back into the house to get Julie and we hurried off to the restaurant and had a good Christmas Eve.

I had put together a Christmas tape with some of the best and worst records ever made, plus a few carols which added a bit of fun... so much fun that we all started to sing along to the carols. Then we pushed a few tables back and started to get those hips moving to Jingle Bell Rock. Julie had invited some of our ski club friends along and spent most of her time with them. My mother, on the other hand, was up giving it her all on our makeshift dance floor. We got to know a lot of the locals that night as they had walked to the restaurant.

The Palm Suite slogan at Christmas

First Christmas at the Palm Suite, 1981

Iver Heath locals showing off their Russian hats on a snowy Christmas

Celebrating Christmas 1981

Christmas at the Palm Suite — all ready for another cocktail-shaking evening

Chapter 5 — Our First Pinewood Studios Dinner

This is probably the most important person who helped change the direction of our destiny and brought us overnight success to the Palm Suite Restaurant. On one of our many empty lunches, just as we were starting to despair, a chap with long, bright red curly hair wearing a cool leather flying jacket and Levi jeans walked into the restaurant. He slowly started to walk around while I was recovering from the shock of someone arriving. He then asked me what the name of the restaurant was. "Oh!" he said, "I am in the wrong place. Not to worry, can I sit here and have lunch?" "Of course," I said and he had one of our hamburgers. He seemed to enjoy it and when he finished, he told me it was a good hamburger but a little overcooked. So, from that day onwards, we asked everyone how they would like it cooked, which certainly helped the popularity of the Palm Suite hamburgers.

I introduced myself and Barbara, the waitress, and he returned the information, introducing himself as David Speed. He had a company at Pinewood, specialising in high-tech special effects. This was great news for us as he was from the studios. He asked if the restaurant was always this quiet at lunches. "Yes, but you have just made it better than yesterday. I don't quite know what to do; if only I could advertise at the studios." He told me not to worry and the word would soon get around the film boys. He then left in a hurry. Would we see him again? Well, the answer was yes! The following lunchtime, he came with his friend who ran Glastonbury music festival (well, that's what he told me anyway) and a couple more work colleagues. The door opened again and a couple more for lunch. They said hello to David, so more film people. David could see I was pleased, and smiled and gave me a wink.

Over the years, lots of studio people have told me they were the first customer from Pinewood, but this makes it official now that it was, in fact, David Speed. I, of course, thank you all for wanting to be the first customer and spreading the word about the Palm Suite.

As I am writing about our first customers, my mother and I had a couple of early favourites; John Dark, a film producer, and his suave organiser and PA, Malcolm Cockren. John was famous for producing many films including the very funny film, *There's A Girl In My Soup* with Goldie Hawn & Peter Sellers. He also produced *Shirley Valentine*, a romantic comedy drama which was nominated and won many awards. This also turned into a London West-End play. I often wonder whether my mother saw herself as a Shirley Valentine while making my father's egg and chips. You will have to watch the film or play to understand that (well worth a view on a cold winter's night). They did make me laugh when they said they should sign our waitress Barbara for their next movie, as she had a natural Marilyn Monroe walk. They did tease her in good fun. Sadly, they never did sign

A rare photograph (not a print) of a young Marilyn Monroe, displayed on the Palm Suite walls for over 25 years

her up so Barbara carried on mopping the Palm Suite floor every morning. Then, one day, she met her Prince Charming and she was gone. Before you accuse me of being the wicked sister, Barbara made a lot of money in tips, keeping all.

The restaurant was now starting to build up a good lunchtime trade and was becoming more and more popular with studio people. Another really good early regular customer was David Ball, who would, when possible, enjoy a long lunch. He seemed to know everyone at the studios and was good at spreading the word secretly about the Palm Suite. At the end of lunch, he would tell me who had been into the restaurant, which often included the top studio bosses. David even designed one of our menu covers. He also gave me several clapper boards and other bits to put on the wall. Then, one day, he told me they were doing a night shoot at Boulters Lock, Maidenhead. This famous bar and restaurant was to be taken over at midnight for a film shoot. David Ball invited me to the set, so, as soon as the restaurant closed that night, I stopped off on my way home. Perfect, as I lived in Maidenhead. I had to find David who was working as production supervisor and was busy giving instructions, talking to lots of people. He suddenly spotted me and called me over, introducing me to the film crew as Dave from the Palm Suite. That's good, spread the word. He then asked me if I wanted a drink, as he had kept the bar open. "Yes, please," and he got me a pint of beer. I noticed most of the crew were working away enjoying a beer or two. This of course would never happen today as drinking is forbidden, and even breathalysers have been threatened. I am certainly not sure if having a sober set ever improved the films.

If you have never seen a film production shoot, they are very exciting as there is a lot of setting up to do. Then there is the big moment when "ACTION" is shouted, followed by "TAKE ONE" and the clapper board bangs together. Total silence is obeyed by all. The actors take over, hoping to get it right first time. The non-filming crew have all frozen waiting for those famous words "CUT". As soon as this happens, everyone talks and the director, camera man, editors etc. discuss the film footage. This was my chance to introduce myself and the Palm Suite Restaurant to the cast, which happened to be the top stars. There was Dennis Weaver, who was Sam McCloud, John Cannon and Melissa Anderson, all starring in this London-based episode of *The Return of Sam McCloud*. No surprises there but I was delighted to get signed pictures which went up in the restaurant.

I left the set at about 4 am feeling very pleased, even though the director told me to stop chatting up Melissa and to get off set. It was a great night.

It was brilliant to meet these three great actors, with an amazing list of performances in various films and television shows

We were becoming more and more popular with the film technical guys and it would be impossible to name them all. I must mention Terry Bamber, who turned out to be probably one of our longest-running regulars. Terry originally trained as an actor at LAMDA, but like his father Dickie, came into the film business. His father worked on the very first Carry On film and Terry worked on the last, *Carry On Columbus*. I am sure that helped make him a very funny actor with so many jokes and one-liners. He is a very popular assistant director and production manager and worked on many James Bond movies. One day, he was in for lunch while shooting the film version of *Phantom of the Opera,* and he invited me to come on set the next day. We arrived at the gate house and signed in, then whizzed off to meet one of Terry's assistants who showed us around the various sets. We were amazed at the costumes and dancing scenes. On our way to Terry's set, we even said hello to Andrew Lloyd Webber who was involved with the film

Many people from the studios have tried to guess the year this picture was taken. We think it is the very hot summer of 1976, hence the very dry grass in this picture. It also shows the 007 stage, which was built in 1976 for The Spy Who Loved Me.

production. Terry was filming some of the eery scenes down under the theatre so it was very dark.

I thought it was very exciting with powerful performances. It shows you what I know, as the film critics disagreed and gave a Rotten Tomato award. I thoroughly enjoyed it at the cinema but this award seems quite common with the odd Pinewood movie. Terry joined us for lunch that day, when, of course, we thanked him. Unfortunately, the afternoon shoot did not go so well for Terry, as a young lad doing some lighting in the rafters fell off, landing on his head. He had been celebrating his birthday at lunch time. Thank God he made a full recovery in hospital; by coincidence, he was the son of one of our cleaners.

Terry was also a great organiser of parties and helped arrange a dinner at the Palm Suite for James Bond film enthusiasts. This involved guest speakers from people who worked on 007 productions. On the other end of the scale, we had a very raucous party that got even louder outside the restaurant. A neighbour called the police and they arrived with dogs. Normally, this would have been enough to quieten any party but not this one. One of the exceptionally loud, very drunk guests decided to kick the police dog, also telling the police where to go. This was not a good idea as he then spent the night in a police cell and Terry had to bail him out the following morning. Not a boring party by any means and not one Terry will forget in a hurry; he was not pleased. We, of course, remained friends.

One of my favourite movies made in 1964. It was filmed on the abandoned sets for Cleopatra in 1963. The costume worn by Sidney James in this film was worn by Richard Burton in Cleopatra. Worth watching, just to see the sets alone and a very funny film!

We also mustn't forget in these male- dominated boozy times, there was a great bunch of sober women helping these guys make these films. They were often PAs and secretaries, and they played a very important part. They would enjoy much shorter lunches but were very good customers, often booking large tables and arranging end-of-shoot parties. I can only remember them by their first names and they were never slow in coming forward, especially the younger ones. Jane would shout at me, often demanding where their meals were if we were running late. I found Jane quite frightening in the early days, but she was a regular for over 25 years. We got on well as years went by and we found her very funny. Lorraine and Dusty in production were all great customers of the Palm Suite, friends of Terry Bamber.

The list of film crew that used our small restaurant round the corner from Pinewood Studios could go on forever. We were very popular with the James Bond crew, particularly the editors headed by John Grover. More about them later, as I have so many great stories about end-of-shoot parties and being taken to lunch at Pinewood. We were also very popular with the special effects departments, and the bosses would often bring about 20 of them down for lunch. This would happen on the spur of the moment and we were lucky to get a phone call to tell us they were on their way. Of course, they wanted one table which meant joining tables together. No problem if no one was sitting on them. The number of times I would be offering drinks on the house to get people to move to a different table in the restaurant. We really had to move it, pouring beers as they arrived, menus on the table ready to go and orders taken in minutes. The chefs were ready to go and as the orders were mainly hamburgers, the kitchen worked very quickly. When my brother was head chef, he would always put the food out in order, making service quicker. We did all this in 50 minutes! The bosses would often stay longer chatting to the

Palm Suite was chosen as the venue for a special event for Bond enthusiasts and the guest speakers included Art Director, Peter Lemont and one of the Directors, Terry Bamber. At the end of the evening, Terry gave me these photographs of the various Bond cars which they used in many of the films.

waitress. One of them, who will remain nameless, used to come in most days for lunch. I thought he really liked our food and drink, but now I know he was actually having an affair with my head waitress. She left and had very successful years financially in the film business. Good for her and the children who joined her.

We never really saw him again, even though we had a picture of him holding his BAFTA award. He also gave me the bolt from the film Event Horizon (a long pointed arrow) which was filmed running down a clear fishing line through a plate glass window, then killing someone… just one of our many film props displayed on the walls. He also gave me an army jacket from the film *Saving Private Ryan*, a great movie. Then he won an Oscar for *Gladiator* so I guess he was pretty good at his job. So, in hindsight, I really don't blame the girl for leaving waitressing at the Palm Suite.

Another chap who, again, was a good regular, gave me the swords from the famous film *Troy* starring Brad Pitt. He also gave me the gold statue's head that stood outside the city of Troy, which Brad Pitt cut off on the film set. He suggested to me I put it on a slow rotating table to display it. I found a company that would do this and they designed it to go in a lit glass box on the rotating table. It looked quite striking when you walked into the restaurant at night-time. Sadly, he is no longer with us, and I am sure will be missed by many including myself.

He was one of the best in special effects and worked on many films including a lot with Jonny Depp. He was very good to me and would invite us to Pinewood for film set tours. The Charlie and the Chocolate Factory sets were very interesting. Then we saw Jonny Depp in action working on a vampire movie, *Dark Shadows*. He also gave my son Daniel work experience and then gave him his first job on *Fast and Furious 6*, a very exciting first job for a lad aged 18.

A busy wall at the Palm Suite, showing the bolt from the film Event Horizon.

One of our early film posters, in an original 1940s cinema frame. Some consider this one of the greatest movies ever made in 1939, and if it's not your cup of tea, it would turn into an endurance test, watching it for 3 hours and 58 minutes!

The Pinewood Studios regular diners loved this photograph, so much so that I went to the printers and bought all their remaining stock!

Chapter 6 — Star-spotting at the Palm Suite

In the early days, I was always saying to the film guys that it would be great if we could get a film star at the restaurant. That would give us a fantastic boost, just one for us to talk about to our slowly growing regular clientele. It was just another Tuesday lunch with a few bookings which suddenly started to grow. This was good, because as we started to fill up, it then happened! Three guys walked in with Mel Gibson (I know I wanted a star to come to the restaurant but wow, I never expected anyone this big!). He was probably one of the biggest up and coming stars on the planet, an A-list star with looks that would make women melt, and we were showing him to a table at the Palm Suite. I was trying to look nonchalant as if we had stars in all the time, the waitress was trembling at the thought of taking his order, and the chef said cooking for famous film stars was not in his contract. "It is now, and you might get a bonus if trade goes up."

I convinced the waitress, who, by coincidence, was only helping us out as Barbara had taken a couple of days off. He was just a regular, friendly guy. Off Anne went to take his order, no problems, as she came back with a beaming smile with his order of swordfish. Probably a good dish to have on the menu for an Australian. We put the order in and we decided not to tell the chef which was his dish out of the four. Good ploy from Anne, but he kept saying, "I bet it's the swordfish." I think maybe the word got around Pinewood that Mel was having lunch at the Palm Suite, as we were very busy. I guess the movie people were used to stars, but outsiders were certainly staring, with a few asking for autographs. He didn't seem to mind and he ate all of his swordfish, which he must have enjoyed as he came back the following lunch for more! The waitress was brave enough to ask him for his autograph and he gave her a signed picture. I always felt it should go up in the restaurant, but telling the evening regulars that Mel Gibson was a regular certainly boosted trade, although it was a slight exaggeration. Well, that was our very first movie star. There were many more to follow, which I will tell you about as we go along.

One Friday evening, I arrived early at the restaurant and the phone came alive with bookings. Then a guy phoned up and said, "I need a table of ten, plus me in half an hour, 6:30 pm. I have a bus full of hungry stars in a rush." Okay, was this a hoax, I thought, but I booked them in and he took my name. Phone goes at 6:30 pm, "Dave, we are still at the studios running late." Twenty minutes later, "Dave we are still running late."

"Get here as soon as you can."

Ten minutes later, "Dave, we are just leaving the studios." By the way, his name was Joe. I don't know what route he took, but twenty minutes later, at 7:30 pm, they arrived.

In they came, the main cast of Stargate. I am sure you have heard of the TV series, but if you were like me at the time, I had never heard of it. It was an incredibly successful film, then turned into a TV series which ran for over 10 years. Their spaceship allowed instant galactic travel, I guess cutting out all the boring bits.

I guess I should have been more star struck than what I was with greeting ten good looking American film stars, but I only recognised a couple. Of course, the staff knew them all. They were good fun and easy to serve, except we had to really speed up as they were late. They mainly had our ribs and hamburgers, which they loved. In fact, Don Davis said to me the BBQ ribs were the best he had ever tasted. He would say to me, "David, I have eaten ribs all over America and I come to England and yours are the best - how do you do it?" Well, later in the book, I will give you the recipe, but buying the right ones from a good butcher is essential.

Joe, their organiser & bus driver, came over to me and complimented the speed and efficiency of the staff and that it was great food. I thanked him and he asked if I wanted any signed pictures to add to our growing collection. Of course I said yes, and pictures and pens were out. Joe handed me six pictures and ushered them all out the door, shouting, "Bye, Dave, see you soon!" Wow, did that really happen… I think the staff and our other customers couldn't quite believe it. So it's now 8:15 pm and back to running a busy Friday night but with lots to talk about.

The TV series ran for 10 years, a jolly long time, with a massive cast list including Amanda Tapping, Michael Shanks, Richard Anderson, Teryl Rothery, Ben Browder, Beau Bridges and Jeff Bridges (brother) to name but a few. I soon framed the photos and put them up together, creating an impressive Stargate line up. Four months later, on a Friday, Joe calls again for another Stargate table of ten stars, some new to the Palm Suite this time, so I would get some more photos signed. Then came the usual calls of running late, booked for 6:30 pm and arriving at 7:30 pm.

They all arrived, this amazing line of stars walking into the Palm Suite, including the very attractive Amanda Tapping. I turned around to the barman who had become star-struck, wide-eyed and gawking at Amanda. "Come on, lads, start making the drinks," I ordered, "as we don't have long." They did stay a little longer this time and I gained another four complimentary signed pictures to add to the collection. The others were so pleased to see their pictures framed in the classic shiny black frame. They left in the usual way, very noisily, saying, "See you next time, Dave," in their American accents. They came another couple of times in their usual way; late, eat, drink and out the door leaving us more pictures to put up. The Stargate cast was a good bonus for the Palm Suite as stars rarely came in for dinner.

It was a real pleasure to meet Ray Winstone one lunchtime, dressed very smartly in a sharply tailored suit. As one of Britain's best gangster actors, he was dressed for the part.

The Cast of Stargate

Although he hasn't always played gangsters, which suits his London Eastend accent, he has a long varied list of films and television appearances. I would have loved to have told you he had a couple fights and left the restaurant threatening to blow it up, but he didn't. Instead, he was very friendly asking questions about the restaurant and the many and various pictures I had up of film stars and television personalities.

He was sitting near the signed picture Stephen Fry who became a regular on Fridays while filming at Pinewood. He was directing his first movie called *Bright Young Things,* which he also wrote based on the novel *Vile Bodies*. Now, before you start thinking this was a horror movie, it is about young and carefree London aristocrats. Stephen Fry's first visit was on a Friday, the restaurant's most popular lunch for fish & chips. We only sold fresh fish and made our own beer batter every morning, which coated the cod making it crisp and light. Most of Stephen's party ordered fish & chips, a dish I was very confident they would like. Stephen Fry is certainly a man that has presence in any room, and enjoyed talking to his guests, as much as they enjoyed listening. Here, we had an interesting articulate gentleman in the Palm Suite, who we all wanted to listen to. Stephen called me over and said the food was delicious and booked for five the next Friday on the same round table. We got that one right and as you have probably guessed, Stephen and I were on first name terms. He came to the Palm Suite another four Fridays and I enjoyed our brief chats each time, often ending the lunch, "See you next week, David," until his last week. When he told me he was heading back to London and asked would I like a signed picture, I immediately said, "Yes please!" I was going to ask that, but the words would never come out as I thought that was something you may not do. We said our farewells and the picture arrived of a good-looking younger Stephen Fry.

The film did very well with a good strong cast, definitely worth viewing and Stephen Fry has a cameo appearance. These cameo roles were probably made famous by Alfred Hitchcock. Which now reminds me of another film-favourite diner, producer Paul Hitchcock, who was no relation to the famous Alfred Hitchcock, but I guess having the same surname was not a hindrance to his career in the movie business. While often having lunch with his P.A. Lidia, he was also making plans to produce more great movies such as *Mission Impossible, The Man in the Iron Mask, Phantom of the Opera* and *Fred Claus*.

Lidia knew I had young children and offered them a tour around the *Fred Claus* sets. The film was based on Santa's naughty brother, and what a great first film set to show them around. This could have sparked their first interest in the film business, which they have gone into, and are starting to build careers in and are all doing well (but, of course, I am the proud father!). While doing a bit of research about Paul Hitchcock's films, I found out since the Palm Suite closed, that he has written a book, *A life Behind the Scenes; from Pinewood to Hollywood*. I have now ordered a copy, which has good reviews and looks like a jolly good read to me. Does Palm Suite get a mention? I was certainly behind the scenes, running Palm Suite, seeing the amount of bad behaviour, often drunken and funny instances I saw over the years. It was always rumoured that Paul was having a relationship with Lidia, who was younger than Paul. She was very attractive and spoke a little like Zsa Zsa Gabor, as she came from an Eastern European country. The book may answer that question! Steve Harding, who helped Paul make these great movies, gave me a pre-screening of the first *Mission Impossible* film - now that was a fantastic perk to having a restaurant next door to Pinewood.

In the eighties and nineties, we had a lot of big named stars that used the restaurant at lunch. I can remember saying one morning, "We haven't had any stars in for ages; what's going on at Pinewood?" Well, I soon found out about an American production called *Loch Ness,* when Ted Danson walked in, famous for the award-winning TV series called *Cheers* and many movies. If you haven't seen it, it's a good time to watch it. It is all about a bar in New York, its ups and downs and is often very funny.

The party asked for a table of six, so we gave them the round table in the centre. They soon relaxed and were eating, drinking and talking about the film. They then left, and I was very surprised how tall Ted was, well over 6ft and with his amazing head of silver hair which made him look even taller. Often you don't see stars again due to shooting schedules, but not in Ted's case, as they were in the next day. They seemed to enjoy the Palm Suite and the food cooked by Rob, my head chef and brother. They came in most lunches over the next few weeks and often chatted to Ted. He often asked me about other film stars that had been in the restaurant, as he did seem to know a lot of them. He was very surprised that Kim Basinger had been in the restaurant while appearing in Batman and had joined an end-of-shoot party. I told him, but he was not as surprised as I was, as she was an Oscar-winning actress in the Palm Suite.

Ted Danson invited me to Pinewood to have a look at the film sets. They were filming in the indoor water tank, which was the cellars under the castle at Loch Ness. We were able to walk around the set, which really felt like you were under a castle. This had water access to the loch so the monster could appear and befriend the little girl who lived in the castle. We then watched the filming of the monster coming out of the water and Dempsey (Ted Danson) shocked to find Isabel (his daughter) talking to it. The little girl was played by a sweet wee young Scottish

lass, who they would bring to lunch with her proud parents. Like all films, the producers were keen to wrap as the cost of filming is very expensive and send their stars home. Their last lunch was now with us and Ted Danson thanked us and complimented our food. Ted gave me a signed picture and I asked the little girl, Kirsty Graham, for a signed picture, which delighted her and her parents. Two more pictures to dress our walls.

The restaurant was quite popular to film in over the years, surprisingly not from Pinewood Studios, but TV comedy and drama programmes. This for me was very interesting, to be involved in a day's shoot, and I learned a lot on how it all works.

The first filming at the Palm Suite was for a French telecoms company. They filmed in the restaurant, the flats above and the car park. They even rented one of the flats for the director and his family, saving them a fortune as they were staying in a luxury hotel nearby. I was very green in those days, as they cleverly did not mention money and I had no idea it was normal to charge a fee. I never made fortunes renting the restaurant, but I always enjoyed it and it was far different from the usual day.

We were often asked to supply breakfast bacon and sausage sandwiches as they arrived, with endless coffee. Some would bring catering vans on the larger productions. There could up to five or six large trucks outside, full up with equipment. The English film industry always uses 'trucks', not lorries - sounds cool, I guess. They would be full of cameras, editing screens, sound equipment and loads of monitors.

If the Palm Suite had been around 10 years earlier, I am sure we would have had the Carry On team filming in the restaurant. Maybe they would have written Carry On Waitressing starring Barbara Windsor as the saucy waitress and Sid James the naughty chef. Palm Suite was a bit of a Carry On at times but they used the houses and gardens in Pinewood Green, and the famous telephone box in many screens. I was given a lot of the Carry On film posters which I would put up in the restaurant. Carry On Cleopatra and Carry On Cowboy were very popular. I had been given old cinema poster display cases so I would rotate the many I got given over the years.

Famous Olympic equestrian Nicola McGivern with the equally famous actor Dustin Hoffman, outside the Palm Suite Restaurant.

This could be set up in the trucks or the tents outside. The clapper board operator would now be in full production, guided by the director as they went through the various screens. Actors were waiting and hoping to get their lines right first time – rare, but sometimes take two or three are worse. Watching cock-ups can be quite amusing, and funny when you get the unexpected swear word.

They rarely wanted the restaurant to look like the Palm Suite, so would change pictures by cutting to size different ones and sticking them over the glass. They dressed the walls and restaurant with different props, so often very different. The most unusual one, which was hilarious, was when they converted the Palm Suite into a lesbian restaurant called *Sappho*. Sappho was the name of a famous female Greek poet who lived on the island of Lesbos. When filming, the attention to detail is essential. Well, this TV drama was no exception, as they produced menus, 'Sappho, Traditional Lesbian Cuisine' with two Victorian naked females on the front cover. They even printed the dishes inside, such as 'Seared Lesbian Scallops £14, Wild Lesbian Salmon with asparagus, sweet lemon and lovage £20, Exotic Lesbian Soufflé £17'. It must have been outrageously funny putting this menu together.

Anyway, believe it or not, they had the famous Suranne Jones starring in it, where they filmed her meeting a lesbian in the restaurant and ordering a meal. I wonder if this inspired her to do the new successful series called *Gentleman Jack,* where she does play an outrageous daring lesbian. I didn't know too much about Suranne Jones as I didn't watch much TV, and Corrie is not my thing. The cast all seemed very relaxed and pleasant as they set up camp in the front of the restaurant on a glorious warm English summer's day.

The filming went well and we finished about 7:30 pm, which wasn't bad as the fee included the evening. They then had to put the restaurant back as they found it, which was rarely achieved. These guys start around 6 am, so the clearing up about 12 hours later (or more) can be hard. Of course, you say they get lots of money, which they might, but I think they definitely earned it.

We never had any warning of any famous actors or actresses coming to the restaurant as I guess they were always concerned we would notify the press in advance. We always followed the strict code that you never reveal anything to the press and so the stars kept coming. The sound department at Pinewood were good regulars, and Glenn Freemantle, an Oscar-winning technician, would often bring in a party for lunch. In the party, on a couple occasions, there was this guy who looked a bit like Dustin Hoffman.

I didn't take too much notice, but he seemed a nice guy like the rest of the party. A couple of regular friends popped in for lunch and joined me at the bar. Then he said, "Big stars in today - Dustin Hoffman." I immediately corrected them, "Just a lookalike; been in before."

"No, David, that really is him!" Unbelievable, as I had managed to convince the staff he was a lookalike. One way to find out was to ask one of the party on the quiet, and they confirmed, "It is Dustin Hoffman." Oh my God, I thought it was a lookalike. Mistaken identity was not the word and my regulars found this hilarious. Nicola had her picture taken with him outside and sent me a copy, and you can see it's the real Dustman Hoffman. Now, if this wasn't bad enough, the light bulb above his head started smoking. I had replaced them all with LEDs at a great cost and this should not be happening. I quickly grabbed a tea towel, pulled up a chair behind where he was sitting, removed the hot bulb and ran outside before he noticed. He must have enjoyed the meal and was pleased everyone had clean plates and paid the bill. We had never seen a star actor pay the bill before.

When he was leaving, we chatted a bit about the restaurant and I told him Jon Voight had also been in the restaurant. They had both starred in the film *Midnight Cowboy* and were both nominated for Oscars. I had played the famous music from the film *Everyone's Talking* by Harry Nelsson. Neither of them had noticed.

Another occasion, I was invited down to the Pinewoods outdoor tank to see some filming. I was rather excited about this as I had never seen this giant outdoor swimming pool before. When I arrived at the studio gates, they told me to drive over and park outside, as it was right over the other side of the studios.

This wouldn't happen today as security is so tight. I parked up nearby, walked around the corner and there was a tank that looked more like a lake with sides. It also had a massive screen for painting the horizon and sky. Over on the other side was a large castle that had been left from the filming of *First Knight* with Sean Connery as King Arthur, and Richard Gere as Lancelot. I was told Sean Connery and Richard Gere did not get on too well, as Sean would bang on his dressing room door telling him to hurry up all the time.

The film I had come to see in production was a surfing movie called *Blue Juice*, starring Sean Pertwee who was playing the top surfer in Cornwall with his girlfriend. His love for his girlfriend is split between surfing and romantic moments, which ends when he hears the big waves are on the way. They were filming surfers in the tank with very choppy water, done by a machine. The cameraman was in the water with some of the crew, all in dry and wet suits. Lifeguards were also on hand. The cast were in swimming costumes and, lucky for them, the water was still warm. Richard Gere had insisted it was heated for him otherwise he was not going in. This was all very exciting, but then I spotted a very famous TV star who must be the girlfriend. It was Catherine Zeta-Jones, famed for her role in *Darling Buds of May*. My word, they were very lucky to have her, considering she now must be one of the top A-listed stars of Hollywood. This low-budget movie couldn't even think of casting her today. Her fee would be more than the whole movie. Unfortunately, I had to get back to the restaurant, but left Inviting everyone to lunch. No cast, or Catherine Zeta-Jones, but the crew came.

Jasper Carrot, who dined with us at both lunch and dinner on the same day

Picture of Sid James, signed by his last wife Valerie

Signed by the director and producers of Cleanskin. Harry Rushton was a regular at the Palm Suite and holds the unofficial record for the longest lunch

The movie business is full of big-talking people, making this film, that film, big budgets, small budgets, all going to become multi-millionaires. They are also after your money, in fact, anybody who will invest in their movie and of course they will make you rich. A lot of movies make enormous sums, but an awful lot lose as well. I think my mother and I are very cautious people and not ones to take risks. Well, that is until we met three guys who became lunchtime regulars, really nice guys enjoying many lunches at the Palm Suite talking movie talk.

They told us about the movie they were going to make about the unlicensed champion bare-fisted boxer, named Lenny McLean. Well, if that didn't sound frightening enough (he was a bouncer and bodyguard), he was friends with the Krays and other Eastend gangsters. He was known as *The Gov'nor,* which was also going to be the title of the film.

Well, I have to say the film sounded great and they had put their own money into it and showed us all sorts of figures, which seemed to all add up. One had a theatre background, the other two were in the film business. They certainly had quite a lot of credentials as one of them, Stanley Sopel, had been Associate Producer on Bond movies and had a good list under his belt. They were very convincing that the film could not fail, so when we were asked if we would like to invest in the film, we were there with our cheque books.

I am not sure how they got involved with Lenny McLean, apart from they mentioned they met him in a restaurant, so I suggested they should bring him to the Palm Suite, to which they agreed. When they met him at Pinewood, they would take him to the restaurant there which always was full of directors & producers in the 80s and 90s. A few days later, in they came with Lenny McLean, and they introduced me - not that I really needed it, as he was big and certainly looked like a boxer. "'Ello Dave," he said in a very deep gruff voice. "Hello, Lenny," my voice also on the deeper side while he gave me one of those hand-crushing shakes. I did my best to exchange a firm hand shake too, but not easy as his hand was twice the size of mine.

The lunch went well and they chatted about the film and money. Lenny chatted to me, asking about the restaurant, how long I had been here and the film star pictures. I refrained from asking about his past, the murder trial at the Old Bailey, where he was found not guilty, I hasten to add, but good really otherwise he would not be sitting in my restaurant. He did used to associate with a lot of Eastend gangsters, including the Kray twins and Charlie Kray, who I met at my friend's restaurant where he was a regular.

There is a common link to why gangsters, CID police and restaurateurs mix, and I think it is their love of food and drink. As the restaurateur, it's very important to remain neutral and not get involved in their business and say nothing. Over the years, I was often told that if I needed any help, to let them know and they would deal with any troublesome, threatening customers causing problems. I never did and remained friends with the right people. Maybe being friendly with these rather tough guys is the reason the Palm Suite never had any trouble or break-ins. Lenny McLean started to use the restaurant quite a bit, driving down from the east end of London, often with friends who looked equally as tough. I told him my mother was an Eastender and he was always very polite and friendly with her. I was born in Greenwich and lived in Deptford and it's a pretty tough place to be brought up. Lenny always said it's the best place in the world to live, but I am not so sure about Deptford. I asked him about a well-known gangster who was on the run in Spain for

Lenny McLean, known as The Gov'nor - this was going to be made into a major feature film starring Craig Fairbrass

five years but had just come back to the UK and handed himself into the police. Lenny said, "As far as I'm concerned, he done time in Spain and now he's got to do another five years here. Probably better than the first five years." From that, I take it he didn't like Spain.

Lenny had a good appetite and would often come into the restaurant and put his big arm around me and say, "Dave, get me some of those chicken bits (Chicken Satay)." He would often eat about three starter portions while waiting for his steak lunch. Lenny didn't drink alcohol, as he said it made him aggressive and he didn't like it anymore. He seemed to become more friendly after a meal, often ordering more chicken bits (Chicken Satay), while chatting to other customers and singing the odd Elvis Presley song.

The film about Lenny, which now had a name, *The Gov'nor,* was making very slow progress and was a little frustrating, as we had invested our hard-earned money into the production. I was starting to think our money was being used to pay for their many boozy lunches. Then Stanley Sopel told us he had some big financial meetings with a far eastern investor, who was keen on the film. The final meeting was just with Stanley at the Palm Suite and it didn't look like it went well. In fact, Stanley left looking like a ruined man and he was, as he had invested every penny he had into the production. His partners had vanished, one of them apparently with the money, so they say.

The last time I saw Lenny McLean at the restaurant, he brought a party of about ten with him and he didn't look happy. He asked me if I had seen Stanley and his mates. I told Lenny the last time was with the film investor. Lenny said, "Those three have got my money and have vanished from Pinewood." The party stayed for a meal and I was introduced to the first Sun newspaper Page 3 girl, which was way back in 1970. Well, she still looked good in the 90s, a nice lady, a real Eastender. They left in a hurry; one of the party, a young woman in her early 20s, had gone out the back and was dancing around the car park. Obviously, they had one too many, but Lenny was not happy and I was seeing the angry side of him. That was his last visit.

Lenny McLean was certainly an interesting person in a different way and was getting more involved in small acting parts in TV and films. Then his big break came in Guy Ritchie's film *Lock, Stock, and Two Smoking Barrels* where he was known as Barry the Baptist, the criminal enforcer. Lenny died in July 1998 shortly before the film was released. Shortly after his death, Lenny's autobiography was published and was soon a bestseller called *The Gov'nor*. This book is still selling well today.

Chapter 7 — Not a Typical Monday Night in the Restaurant

It was a cold damp night outside, but the restaurant was warm and cosy and starting to get busy. Monday nights were always popular with families, and one of our waitresses had booked a table of twelve, mainly children, for a birthday. The restaurant looked more like a kindergarten play school. The noise was high with the chatter of kids, about thirty of the lovely little darlings running around the restaurant, not one of the parents taking the slightest bit of notice.

I had busy staff; the chefs were turning their culinary skills to our children's menu and the food was flying out. The coffee machine was going. Waiters and waitresses were dodging kids serving the meals. The barman was busy making mocktails (non-alcoholic colourful cocktails).

I was showing a couple of guys to the corner table away from the chaos. The had asked if they could have a quick meal as they were working down at the studios. This was a common request and not a problem, and I asked what film they were on as I gave them the menus. "*Gulliver's Travels,*" said the one that looked very familiar. "Kids movie?" I asked. "No shortage of them round here, so sorry about the noise." But what noise? As I walked away from the table, I couldn't help but notice the restaurant had become quieter, a lot quieter. They were sitting huddled together at their tables all looking over to the corner table. The parents were still not noticing a thing, still chatting, eating and drinking.

I proceeded to the bar and could hear them murmuring Jack Black and of course this was confirmed by my younger staff. "You mean the guy who did *School of Rock*, the one in the film poster on the wall? That's so cool! Thought it was him." Owners are allowed the odd lie.

This then interested the parents, with the children getting excited again, and parents asking me if I thought he would do some autographs. One of the waitresses had already made sure she was going to take his order and, of course, sneaked in his autograph on her waitress pad. The request for more autographs was easy as he didn't mind at all.

The next thing I knew, we had an orderly queue all around the restaurant to meet Jack Black and get his autograph. I have to say he was great and the most obliging film star I had ever met. As there were so many children, we had to stop while they ate their Cheese & Bacon Burgers. He then finished the signing.

Film stars seem to like meeting owners of restaurants, probably as we are good at making them feel special, and we are showmen and show women running our business. So,

I popped over to his table to thank him for his impromptu signing session. They told me they had hoped to practice some lines over dinner, but the kids were more fun. I pointed out that we had the School of Rock film poster up in the restaurant and asked if he would sign it for us. He replied, "Eating your great hamburgers, it will be my pleasure. Send it down to Pinewood." With that, they left with a quick wave and goodbye to everyone.

I took the poster out of the display box and sent it down to the studios. The next day, it came back with the most amazing compliment the restaurant had ever had. "To all at the Palm Suite, David, your Hamburgers Rock."

Thank you, Jack! That's the best endorsement I could ever wish for; as good as winning a Michelin Star.

Chapter 8 — I Met John Malkovich

The title sounds like a sequel to *Being John Malkovich,* which is the name of one of the great movies he has made. In fact, he has appeared in about 90 films now and has produced and directed many.

I met John Malkovich one lunch time while he was working on a film called *Mary Reilly* played by Julie Roberts. *Mary Reilly* was Dr Jekyll's housekeeper and, of course, Mr Hyde's when he popped in. I don't often meet stars in full film costume and, even more surprisingly, dressed as a Victorian Dr Jekyll. He politely ask if he was alright in his film outfit.

I told him he looked very smart and it was no problem. He ordered a large wine and told me he had a bad morning on set with one of the female stars who was proving to be very difficult to work with, mentioning no names, of course.

John Malkovich became quite a regular and would often bring his wife and children in the early evening. He had hired a car and was soon parking behind the restaurant and coming in through the back door. By this time, we were on first name terms and he often asked me to sit at their table after the meal. He was very interested in the running of the restaurant and the kitchen. Now that I know he owns a restaurant in Lisbon called *Bica do Sapato*, I can understand his interest. Great restaurant, I can definitely recommend it. I, of course, was more interested in his film career at the time.

John Malkovich in costume filming 'Mary Reilly' 1996

Another thing I remember about John Malkovich was that he never wore socks, which I found strange, but it is very fashionable now so not only is he a good actor, director & producer, but he is a fashion trendsetter - a very interesting guy who is definitely on my dinner party list. He gave me a signed picture before he left Pinewood, which I placed by my favourite table. Unfortunately, I don't think *Mary Reilly* will be one of his favourite films and joined the list of Pinewood Studios films not talked about, getting a rotten tomatoes rating of 26%!

George Cole was also in this film, a man who is probably more fondly remembered for his role in the TV series *Minder*, which was sometimes filmed at Pinewood. Palm Suite was a favourite haunt of the film crew, led by a great chap called Ken. They would go out on recces, which means they got out of the studios to find a new filming location. This, of course, would always involve lunch at Palm Suite on their return to Pinewood. Not where they were supposed to be.

They noticed I had a very old picture of a young George Cole when he starred in a film called *The Constant Husband*. They asked if they could borrow it to make George a Christmas card from them. This I agreed to, but only if they could ask him to sign it. They gave George the Christmas card, signed from the crew, and told him that the picture had been hanging on the Palm Suite Restaurant walls for years. He signed the picture, but he never joined the crew to see it back up in the restaurant.

A very young George Cole starring in 'The Constant Husband' in 1955

Chapter 9 — The Avengers

Now, you are probably thinking of that bunch of unusually dressed crusaders who go around saving us from various monsters. No, this was not the big epic film, but the frightfully British one based on the 1960's TV series. The 60's version starred Patrick Macnee as John Steed, topped with a bowler hat and armed with an umbrella.

Emma Peel was his accomplice, dressed in a leather figure-hugging catsuit. This was the 60s and so successful that they went on and did a new series in the 1970s starring Joanna Lumley as Purdey, called *The New Avengers*. I have never met a Purdey, but Joanna Lumley did come in for lunch. I wanted to ask why they called her Purdey, which seems now like a ridiculous cat-like name, that sounds very sexist. I thought better of it, but maybe it enhanced her very successful career.

This film version of *The Avengers* with its heavyweight cast had chosen Pinewood Studios as its main location. This was good news for Palm Suite, as the Producer Jerry Weintraub & Director Jeremiah Chechik and crew started to enjoy lunch with us. A lot of the film crew seemed very weary of Jerry, probably as he had threatened to break someone's legs. Jerry seemed to get on with us and he would often pop in for supper with his P.A. and companion, Susan Ekins who was *The Avengers* executive producer.

Things were going extremely well at the restaurant and what a fantastic job I had being near to Pinewood. As we set up for lunch, a large, suited chap came in looking around, then booked a table for two that lunch. Nothing unusual, until they arrived and I found myself showing Ralph Fiennes & Uma Thurman to a table. These award-winning stars were having lunch at the Palm Suite. This was exciting and I had been told that if you meet Ralph Fiennes, you pronounce his name Rafe. He hates being called Ralph. I opted for Mr Fiennes & Ms Thurman and delightfully, Uma said, "Please, Uma is fine" and Ralph said the same. They told me they were working on a film together and how frightfully British they had to be. Not so easy for Uma, I guess. Well, that certainly broke the ice for me and their lunch went well. The waitresses gossiped a bit, suggesting they were on a date. If they were, we never saw Ralph again, but Uma became a lunchtime regular.

Film crews were great ones for passing on gossip and would always tell you not to tell anyone. They assured me Uma & Ralph didn't get on well on or off the set. The lads loved Uma and nicknamed her 'The Body', Probably because of the Emma Peel's tight leather catsuit customs. To add to her many attributes, I must agree she had a very good figure.

As the filming of *The Avengers* was drawing to a close, I thought it would be a great idea to ask Uma for a signed picture before the production finished. I always got a bit nervous asking, but it came out as, "Dare I be so bold as to ask you for a signed picture?"

"Thank you, David, I am most flattered you have asked; of course." The next day, I had a signed picture and one from Ralph Fiennes too. They were framed and up in the restaurant in days, but I decided not next to each other.

This was another great movie for the Palm Suite. Unfortunately, that can't always be said about the films produced at Pinewood. This one turned out to be a bit of a stinker, as it was a box office bomb winning a Rotten Tomato Rating of 5.

This film couldn't be saved, even by Sean Connery, who plays the dastardly villain Sir August De Winter, who is out to destroy the weather. I would have thought England does a good job of that most summers anyway. Sean Connery's part was very small, enabling him, apparently, to spend most of his time at Stoke Poges Golf Club. This unusually bad movie also stared Eddie Izzard, the rather different comedian and actor who brought about a very amusing lunchtime at the Palm Suite, chatting to many of the diners. I can remember being rather fascinated by his black fingernails, not knowing that he liked ladies' clothing. I should have asked for a signed picture as he went on to become very famous for his outrageous dressing and humour.

Jerry Weintraub never returned to Pinewood but did go on to produce *Ocean's Eleven* and many more great movies.

You may now recognise Ralph Fiennes as the new M in the latest James Bond films

Chapter 10 — For Your Eyes Only and the James Bond Film Crew

The first 80's James Bond movie, *For Your Eyes Only,* was released the same month as Palm Suite Restaurant opened in June 1981. We had a budget of £32,000, while theirs was $28 million and the film took a staggering $195.3 million. Whilst we barely broke even in our first year, our luck was soon to change as with their success, Eon productions booked Pinewood Studios in 1982 for the next Bond film.

It didn't take the film crew long to find the Palm Suite and discover our hamburgers and cocktails. We became very popular with the editorial and art departments run by John Grover and Peter Lamont. Soon after, director John Glen and producer Albert Broccoli were also using the restaurant.

The title of a film is usually top secret and often called something different while filming. I was soon told the next James Bond movie was going to be called *Octopussy* and was to be released in June 1983. Not a bad turnaround for a film which started in August 1982. It's a tradition to have an end-of-shoot party and we had a lot from the James Bond film department over the years. *Octopussy* was our first party so we were very keen to get it right. We planned a three-course meal and everybody pre-ordered for speed of service.

A choice of wine and a drinks budget was agreed but it was never stuck to, which certainly added to the fun. About a week before the party, I was asked if I would organise a singing telegram for their producer "Cubby" Broccoli. This had suddenly got very popular in the UK and you could have a choice of costumes that the song would be sung in. I contacted a London company and passed on details for the jingle to be composed for "Cubby" and about his film. The crew chose a scantily dressed young lady in a black corset with suspenders and stilettos. Saucy and suggestive and nothing more. Price agreed, song approved and I had to pick her up from Uxbridge tube station on the day.

The guests started to arrive at the restaurant at about 12:00 pm for champagne and sat at 1:00 pm for the meal. It was all going well, so I nipped off to pick up the singing-telegram lady. We had no mobile phones in those days so had to describe myself and the car, a Ford Capri GT. I was outside the station when suddenly, in jumped a very attractive girl introducing herself as Samantha.

As we were heading back, she asked me where she should get changed. I suggested the stock room back at the restaurant. I could tell she was not impressed and said my car was a better alternative and did I mind. Of course I did think she would wait until we got back. Not the case! Car seat went back and clothes being removed.

This is an editing machine, given to the restaurant by John Grover. This edited a lot of the James Bond films in the 80s.

Within a couple of minutes, I was driving next to a nearly naked woman, not the easiest thing to do and I got a few surprised looks at the traffic lights and I asked her to duck down. On with the corset, black stockings and the high heels. That was some drive!

We parked up and in Samantha went with a large coat on. I pointed out "Cubby." Holding the hand-written telegram, she went over while removing her coat and plonked herself on his lap and sang the song, which finished with huge applause from everyone. He took it in really good spirits and it was a lot of fun. The film lads were very impressed with Samantha and I think they were trying out a few of the new James Bond lines on her. She stayed around and had a couple of drinks.

I drove her back to Uxbridge station in her normal clothes, having got changed in the restaurant's ladies'. I then clumsily asked her out for dinner, but she sweetly declined. How could she with my connections in the film business? I may even be the next James Bond; after all, this was Roger Moore's 6th film and he went on to do another, making a total of 7. Of course, I was never asked to be James Bond, but they did ask me to do the next end-of-shoot party for *A View To A Kill*.

It was quite an honour to be asked again and a real compliment, as we must have got it right back in 1983 when they completed *Octopussy*. I must point out this is not the main large end-of-shoot party where everyone is invited who worked on the film, which would go into hundreds of cast and crew. This party was for the last of the crew still working on the film, including producers Albert R. Broccoli, Michael G. Wilson and director John Glen. The person who organised these parties was the Unit Manager, Production Office, Iris Rose who joined Eon Productions in 1980 for the filming of *For Your Eyes Only*. Iris would write to me on James Bond 007 letter headed paper, confirming the lunch details, called the 'Dubbing Lunch.'

I am so pleased I saved these letters showing the menu and details of the lunch. We would put together this 3-course menu and Iris Rose would get everyone's order. The most popular dish was fillet steak. Iris would even get their wine preference. The crew chose our most expensive French wines but still a lot cheaper than most other restaurants. Again, I will boast the lunch was as successful as Roger Moore's last Bond movie, which was maybe not his best. In fact, he and some of the other cast members didn't like the film.

During the making of Bond movies, the crew of various departments would have lunch at least a couple of times a week at the Palm Suite. I was now on first name terms with a lot of the crew, which was good. I was chatting to a lot of the editors one lunch and they asked me if I had ever had lunch at Pinewood. When I said no, I hadn't, they immediately said, "You must join us and see the competition". So, a couple of days later, I drove down to the gates at Pinewood and, with my name on the guest list, was told where to park. I then found the editing department. This was not that glamorous, in fact, rather untidy bits of

Happy 21 years in films Cubby Broccoli!

There's No Broccoli like Cubby Broccoli
Like No Broccoli we know
Everything about him is appealing
So the people here would like to say
That they want to send him many greetings
And hope he'll celebrate 21 years in films today!

There's No Producer like this Producer
At his work he's truly the tops!
It's said that Cubby used to be a farmer
And in his garden truck he did go far
But something else out there was calling him
And from farming to filming guided his lucky star!

There's No Boss like this Boss
To all his Co-Workers he's the best!
They've worked on many James Bond films together
And Octopussy was a lot of laughs
It's going to be the biggest success yet
And reap dollars! — though Cubby is no good at Maths!

There's No Party like this Party
You're Celebrating in style
The people here would dearly like to have it said
That they toast your health for the years ahead
And let me add right now — with no more further ado
You're dynamic — you know it's true
So dearest Cubby — Congratulations to you!

Love from all de film Crew X

The original hand-written singing telegram

ALBERT R. BROCCOLI
presents
ROGER MOORE
as IAN FLEMING'S
JAMES BOND 007
in
A VIEW TO A KILL

PRODUCED BY ALBERT R. BROCCOLI AND MICHAEL G. WILSON SCREENPLAY BY RICHARD MAIBAUM AND MICHAEL G. WILSON DIRECTED BY JOHN GLEN

PLEASE REPLY:
C/O PINEWOOD STUDIOS,
PINEWOOD ROAD,
IVER,
BUCKS. SL0 0NH
TEL. IVER (0753) 651700
TELEX 849091 EON G

Mr. David Williams,
Palm Suite Restaurant,
52 St. Davids Close,
Bangors Road North,
Iver Heath,
Bucks.

26 April, 1985

46.
+1

Dear Mr. Williams,

Further to Tom Pevsner's letter of 24 April, we are now able to let you have the numbers for selected items from your Menu, as follows:

To Start	Prawn Cocktail	~~25~~ ~~26~~ 27
	Beef Sate	~~16~~ ~~18~~ 19
To Follow	Prime Fillet Steak	~~25~~ ~~31~~ 32
	Gourmet Chicken	~~7~~ 8
	Barbecue Spare Ribs	~~7~~ 8
	French Fries	21
	Jacket Potatoe	23
	Salad	21
Palm Sweeties	Butterscotch Monday	~~19~~ 20 21
	Toasted Waffle	~~13~~ 12
	American Cheesecake	10 ✓
	Cheese & Biscuits	1
Wines	Red	~~15~~ 13
	White	~~26~~ 23
	Beer	1
	Soft Drinks	3

For the wines we have selected Beaujolais Villages A.C. for the red and Macon Villages A.C. for the white. Although we have had responses from 43 regarding drinks, 7 did not indicate any preference.

At the moment we are anticipating 52 will need to be seated, but are awaiting replies from five of them to confirm to us that they can come. I will let you know next week when we hear further from them and what their selected Menus are.

We will have to arrange it so that when everyone is seated your waitresses for the respective tables will take the orders from those they are serving, and we assume they will all remember what they ordered! I could, of course, issue everyone with small white cards with their individual Menus typed on for them to give to their waitresses, but it would I fear make it

(continued)

One of the many food orders from the end-of-shoot parties that we did!

film lay everywhere, with film splicing and editing machines that you turned by hand so you could see it frame by frame. Peter and John said they would show me bits of the film after lunch.

We then headed to the main building and entered a large ornate room with chandeliers. On the right was a very large hot buffet displaying various dishes, hot and cold, with film crew and cast queuing, holding plates ready to help themselves. In the queue that day was Roger Moore, chatting with other cast and crew. The seating was a mixture of large bench-like tables with long chairs, so everyone and anyone could all sit together when it was busy. You could be sitting next to Roger Moore or even a Bond girl, or so Peter told me. Peter was the young good-looking editor who had a reputation for chatting up the girls. He gave me a picture of himself, surrounded by various Bond girls, which he wanted me to put up in the restaurant. I never did though as I was advised not to.

We got our food and I chose a roast as John had recommended, and which most seemed to have. I sat on one of the large tables with others from the editing department who were all chatting about the film. John asked me what I thought of the restaurant and the food. I have to say I was very surprised it was a buffet, but it worked for the hundreds of meals they had to serve in one hour and the food wasn't bad. They assured me it wasn't always good and fish & chip Friday was the best day. That was a handy tip and was the start of the Palm Suite's Cod Fish & Chips Friday, that would come in fresh that morning. We served it with peas, then mushy peas as requested by Jasper Carrot, then both as not everybody agreed with Jasper.

We finished the lunch and they kindly paid for me and invited me back to the editing department to view some of the new Bond movie, *A View To A Kill*. This was very exciting and I could only be the envy of all those millions of Bond fans around the world. John showed me what they were working on and how they edited the film, taking out frames, replacing sections and creating a good flow. Peter asked John whether they could show me the out-takes. He agreed but swore me to secrecy as *It Will Be Alright On The Night* had been after these film clips for years.

They loaded up their secret film of out-takes and told me to look down the viewfinder. It started with the usual music and Bond walking up to the circle with gun in hand, then Roger Moore turns around, pulls his trousers down and moons through the circle. Then we went into a very fast train scene with Bond hanging on the outside fighting a villain. Very exciting until a fault occurred on the fast running background and it stopped, leaving them just standing on boxes on the side of the train. The wind machine was still running, blowing their hair, then it was cut and everyone started to laugh - including Roger Moore. Apparently, Roger Moore was well-known for his pranks and larking around. They showed me a few more out-takes then they knuckled down to some more serious editing. That was some lunch.

The dubbing lunch for *A View To A Kill* went well although their numbers rose to 52 and as we only sat 48 in those days, it meant it was a bit of a squeeze. Nobody seemed to mind as they tucked into fillet steak all cooked to their liking, no mean feat for the chefs - 32 steaks in total. The BBQ ribs and gourmet chicken were easy dishes and cooked quickly, so they all ate together. After desserts, it was time for the brandies and liqueurs. Then, as a Cubby Broccoli tradition, he would hand out his favourite very expensive Panama Cigars and about 30 of them lit up.

The restaurant soon became very smoky, resembling a London smog. I was at the bar and the top table was starting to disappear. The chefs had gone and turned off the extraction. I made it to the kitchen and got the extraction on, so the smoke soon disappeared through the large kitchen hatch. Thank God most of us smoked in those days.

The next 007 film had to have a new James Bond after Roger Moore's retirement. This caused a certain amount of excitement and speculation by the press on who it was going to be. Pierce Brosnan, who was a favourite, was unavailable. It was finally announced it was going to be Timothy Dalton, who I had never heard of at the time. He had started his career in television, then was mainly a theatre actor in the 1970s. He did a lot of classic-type films: *Wuthering Heights*, *Cromwell*, *The Vortex* and *Mary Queen of Scots*. So, to become a James Bond was a very different style of film and the first was called *The Living Daylights*. The filming went very well, with the producers and directors confident it was going to be another success.

This was extremely good for the Palm Suite, as Iris Rose booked their now called 'The Bi-Annual Dubbing Lunch.' This time it was arranged that they would bring their own Bollinger Champagne, which would arrive chilled at 12:45pm. The driver would then take a fillet steak meal back to the studios for the chief sound man who had to remain on duty. It was a pleasure to arrange these parties with Iris Rose, as her attention to detail was second to none. The menu chosen this year had their usual fillet steak, rump steak, chicken chasseur and our new hot smoked trout. The trout was hickory-smoked in our new American smoking oven. Cubby Broccoli chose this dish and, having eaten all of it, I asked him what he thought of it. Not quite the reply I was expecting - "Yes, very interesting." It did sound like a line from a 007 movie, but it left me confused over his enjoyment of the meal.

The afternoon went well and the crew were getting very jolly and nobody seemed in a rush to leave. I had instructions only to serve one liqueur after the meal and afterwards, they had to buy their own drinks if they wanted another. I, of course, checked with the remaining organisers whether I should close the bar for Eon Productions. He said, "I don't think anyone wants anymore to drink but leave it open". He was wrong there, as they started to knock them back. They then told me to close the bar and left the party shaking hands and saying their goodbyes. It was now 6 pm and we were letting our evening diners in, most going to the private cinema, Club 7. They were rather surprised to see a large table of rather drunk people. I of course, told them it was the top crew from the 007 movie, which they had just finished filming. They were slowly picked up and the restaurant slipped into its usual busy Friday night, finishing around midnight. My staff and I were knackered as we had started around 9 am that morning. That was our third 007 movie party and we were very pleased as the crew had a good time. The movie was very successful, grossing more than the last two, so Timothy Dalton was warming for the next James Bond.

The next 007 movie was *Licence To Kill,* which progressed well at Pinewood Studios and the Palm Suite took the booking for our 4th Dubbing Lunch. Iris Rose wrote to me with her usual efficiency, giving all the details which were now fairly similar to the last do. The exception to this Bond movie was that it was going to be released in the summer blockbuster season. Unfortunately, the BBFC (British Board of Film Censors) gave this 007 film a 15 certificate. This was bad news, which reflected in the mood of the crew on their arrival at the Palm Suite as this had just been announced. This stopped all those 12-to-15-year-old children from viewing the film at the cinema. It didn't take long before they all cheered up after a few glasses of champagne. The 15 certificate could seriously affect box office sales and then the release dates turned out to be the same time as other blockbuster films. The eventual result was that the film did not take the many more millions that they wanted, but it still made a substantial profit.

We were very pleased with how the lunch went and this was confirmed when I received a letter on 007 paper thanking me and the staff. The letter also said that they hoped to do it again in 2 years' time, but before then, they had to work hard and make another Bond movie. This wasn't meant to be as there were a lot of delays, although they started pre-production in May 1990, but it was then cancelled causing further problems. Timothy Dalton decided to retire from the role in 1994.

A new James Bond had to be found and this time Pierce Brosnan took the role. Good news we thought at the Palm Suite but not the case as Pinewood Studios was full up. The famous 007 set was being used and with offices scarce, a new location base had to be found. The Leavesden Flight Centre, which had been previously owned by Rolls Royce, was found by Eon Productions with Peter Lamont and they thought it would be ideal to film the next 007 film, *GoldenEye*. This enormous task was given to Peter Lamont to convert the one-million-square-foot factory into a film studio, as well as designing the new film sets.

Peter Lamont and his family lived locally to Palm Suite and was one of our favourite regulars, as he had used the restaurant since we opened. He would often have time to talk to me about the Bond films and invited me to have lunch with him at the new Leavesden Studios. This was very exciting and he gave me a complete tour of the site, showing me the various parts they had used for filming *GoldenEye*. This film was an immense success afterwards and accumulated a worldwide gross of over $350 million. This secured the future of 007 movies after all the upsets and a six-year gap.

ALBERT R. BROCCOLI
presents
TIMOTHY DALTON
as IAN FLEMING'S
JAMES BOND 007
LICENCE TO KILL

PRODUCED BY ALBERT R. BROCCOLI AND MICHAEL G. WILSON WRITTEN BY MICHAEL G. WILSON AND RICHARD MAIBAUM DIRECTED BY JOHN GLEN

Please reply to
Eon Productions Ltd.
Pinewood Studios
Pinewood Road
Iver, Bucks. SL0 0NH, England.
Tel: (0753) 651700
Fax: (0753) 656383
Telex: 849091 EON G

Mr. David Williams,
Palm Suite Restaurant,
52 St. Davids Close,
Bangors Road North,
Iver Heath,
Bucks.   7 June, 1989

Dear David,

    Many thanks indeed for the breakdown of your bill, which is necessary for our auditors or whoever else inspects the books occasionally! We have pleasure in enclosing our cheque for £1,405 in payment for the Lunch specially arranged for us on Friday, 12th May.

    Needless to say, it was once again an excellent meal and everyone appreciated your hard work in making it a most pleasant event.

    We all hope to do it again in two years' time, but before then I am afraid we have to work hard to make another Bond picture. Our new film seems to be well received by everyone who has seen it so far, but of course only the Box Office and the general public worldwide will confirm our optimistic hopes for a success.

    Please thank all your staff for their work at our Lunch, and generally for making things so friendly in your restaurant.

                Yours sincerely,
                 For Eon Productions Ltd.

                 Iris Rose
                 Unit Manager – Production Office

Unfortunately, due to the relocation, they did not have the usual end-of-shoot dubbing lunch at the Palm Suite. This ended a long tradition of 007 movie parties, but it didn't stop any of the film crew from coming to the Palm Suite, and one evening, they brought Pierce Brosnan in for a meal and a few beers. It was very easy to see why he had been chosen for the part; stylish, good-looking, friendly and he was one of the boys and drank beer. He went on to do four 007 movies and was the only James Bond to dine at the Palm Suite. He gave me a signed picture, looking very cool in his dinner suit. Now, that helps business and was certainly noticed by our customers, as they used to ask us what he was like.

"TOMORROW NEVER DIES" Keith Hamshere

Chapter 11 - No Sinking Feeling About These Movies

Peter Lamont went on to do many more Bond movies and slipped in one of his greatest achievements to win an Oscar for his work on Titanic (1997 film). This was fantastic for the Palm Suite, and on Peter's return from Hollywood, he brought in his Oscar to show us. This was early on a Saturday night when the restaurant was full and everybody was so incredibly interested and wanted to hold it. Photos were being taken and customers were asking Peter how he'd won it and about the film. I think the award went around the restaurant and back where I had my picture taken with Peter holding his Oscar. I can tell you the real Oscar is very heavy. That was a good night at the Palm Suite and especially for our customers being able to hold a real Oscar and have a picture taken.

In fact, there have been only just over 3,000 Oscars ever won since 1929 so to have a real one in our small restaurant in Iver Heath is pretty special. We did have a copy Oscar statuette which some guy had made at Pinewood. He said he had got hold of the original mould and was selling them and this was his last one so he had saved it for me. I won't tell you what I paid for it, but now that I have held the real thing, I was done. It wasn't even the right colour gold. Silly me.

Peter brought a friend of his in, Charles, who he had worked with on the Titanic film. He asked me to look after him as he would be dining with us most evenings on his own while he was working at Pinewood. He was a nice chap, so it was no effort for myself or staff to chat to him. After a couple of months, he told me his contract had ended and tomorrow was going to be his last night. When he came in, he gave me a large box and told me to open it. Inside was a Titanic film poster signed by Kate Winslet & Leonardo DiCaprio. My eyes widened and Charles said, "For you. Thank you for looking after me." This was one of my favourite posters that was often displayed in the restaurant.

Pinewood Studios has been a popular venue for making movies worldwide, but not all of them get the right funding. Producers could withdraw finance often as they didn't feel the movie would be successful. This was perhaps an easy get out which would often leave crew unpaid having put in weeks of work. I have seen a few sad faces in the restaurant for this reason, as they knock back a drink or two. "No reason to go back to work, Dave," they would say. "Pour us another one" (a popular movie phase).

The Pinewood movie that seemed to have a bit of a rocky time but just kept going, probably due to Warner Brothers and the director Stanley Kubrick, was *Eyes Wide Shut*. This was certainly a good movie for Palm Suite, as a lot of the crew would be in daily for lunch. They even talked me into doing breakfast, which we had never done before. This certainly

One of my favourite posters signed by the stars!

Peter Lamont
Production Designer for Titanic

appealed to the construction guys who would order their choice of cooked breakfast each morning and we would have it ready for the break at 10:00 am. Those were certainly long days as my brother Rob and l would start at 7:00 am and often wouldn't finish until midnight.

Production started on the film in 1996 and it was released in 1999, over 2 years in the making. It was taking so long that Tom Cruise and Nicole Kidman moved here. The movie also holds the record for the longest continuous film shoot… 400 days. You wouldn't think a film about sexual relations and orgies would take that long to make.

One of the locations was Highclere Castle, which was used for the less dignified scenes including an orgy. Some years after the *Eyes Wide Shut* film was released, we had the pleasure of meeting Lady Carnarvon whose home is Highclere Castle. We discussed the film and I mentioned that it was very good for my restaurant being so close to Pinewood Studios. "Well," she said, "it was good for Highclere but the film should have been called *Legs Wide Open*." I certainly chuckled at the amusing remarks.

This great movie was made by Stanley Kubrick and released in 1987. I felt very privileged to be given this poster as Stanley Kubrick himself had signed it.

Chapter 12 - Holy Hollywood, Batman's Being Filmed at Pinewood!

We were all surprised and delighted at Palm Suite that this great American icon had chosen Pinewood. I guess, as Gotham City doesn't exist, it could be built anywhere. This turned out to be one of the largest film sets ever built. Production started on *Batman* in 1988, starring Jack Nicholson, Michael Keaton and Kim Basinger.

The Palm Suite soon became popular with the production guys, probably helped by Steve Harding and Les Tomkins who were directors on *Batman* and also regulars at the restaurant. We also had the director of photography, Roger Pratt, dining regularly with Terry Gilliam of the Monty Python fame. I am not too sure of Terry's involvement in *Batman* but he has directed and produced lots of movies, so I am sure they were using his expertise.

As the movie progressed, Roger and Terry asked me if they could do an end-of-shoot party just for the filming guys on the last day of the shoot. They expected to finish at 3:30 pm after our lunch. I had never catered for a party at that time but agreed to it. We arranged a hot and cold buffet for about 50 people and they could have the restaurant until 6:00 pm, so that we could do our usual early dinners.

The film business is renowned for running late and it was 4:30 pm when they started to arrive. We soon got the party going, with the drinks flowing and hot ribs, chicken and burgers coming from the kitchen. We were off to a good start and then Roger & Terry arrived, apologising for being late, and gave me the last *Batman* clapper board of the day and film. Now, that is some present. It was displayed above a full-size *Batman* poster in the restaurant.

The party was going smoothly and it seemed all the crew had arrived and were enjoying themselves, chatting about the film. Then, an extra couple of guests arrived and came to the bar to order drinks. This including a young lady wearing a baseball cap. As I asked what she would like, I realised who it was… Kim Basinger, so I immediately did my 'hello and welcome to the Palm Suite'. She got her drink and then happily went to the party to mingle. I was annoyed I never asked for a signed picture, but she was busy and then we were saying our goodbyes.

The film went on to be a massive success, taking millions of dollars at the box office. I was also given a fantastic picture of the Batmobile which we had up in the restaurant. It turned out that one of our regular customers had designed the very big car, so I asked him if he would sign the picture. He did, along with his two designer colleagues who had put the car together. Another prize procession for us to display.

BATMOBIL 1989
DESIGNED AND MADE BY ANTON FURTS, TERRY ACKLAND-SNOW
ENGINEERED BY JOHN EVANS

It was now 6:30 pm and our evening clientele were arriving, so we were slowly getting the restaurant back together as the party left. Roger and Terry said goodbye to the staff, then paid and tipped them well. I thanked them for holding their party at the Palm Suite.

As it was a Friday, a lot of the diners were going on to Pinewood Club 7, the studio's film club, which was excellently run by Dee Knight. They were very interested in the film party, so we were telling them all about it and about meeting Kim Basinger. We had a lot of regulars from the film club who used to run every Friday, Saturday & Sunday. In fact, a lot of the club members would book their film tickets and then phone me to book tables for 3 months. Good business for both Dee and myself. Our working relationship was so good that I would phone Dee and asked her to hold the running of the film, as regular film-goers were running late at the restaurant. We would get early and late diners and the late ones would tell us about the film and normally rate it for us.

The staff and I had many favourite diners from the Pinewood Club 7, but the worst was one who would always moan about the lighting, loud music and other clientele, especially children. Then, one day, when she accused me of not serving her Dover Sole and that it was some cheap alternative, she refused to pay for it. I was starting to hate this woman and seriously wanted to ban her. Luckily, she did not appear on my weekend work evenings for some weeks, so banning her was forgotten.

Unfortunately, Dee Knight, who had been running Pinewood Club 7 for a number of years, was asked to leave the studios when the lease ended in 2013. This was a devastating blow for Palm Suite, as, in our remaining years, we were never able to fill the gap of the Pinewood Club 7 diners. This was a very sad moment, as the club had been running for over 40 years; myself and the staff watched many great movies there. They formed anther club, but it was never the same.

Chapter 13 - Saturday Night's Alright For Fighting

We only ever had one fight in the restaurant and it was on a Saturday night when we were very busy. This was only a couple of punches really, but enough to cause quite a stir in the restaurant.

There was a table of 4 booked at 9:00 pm. Their table wasn't ready when they arrived, so it was drinks at the bar to start and all was going well. One of the couples were regulars and the other was his old school buddy and wife, whom he hadn't seen for a few years. His friend was quite moody, didn't know what to drink and, at the table, wasn't sure what to eat. We helped him along and took an order, but we weren't sure if that's what he actually wanted.

The starters arrived and were eaten, then they finished a couple of bottles of wine. The main course arrived and he said he hadn't ordered that dish. They all said he did (including his wife), but he was not having it, when suddenly, our regular customer shouted at his old friend, "I have had enough!"

Both stood up and blows started. The old school friend took a punch firmly on the chin. He fell backwards onto the round table in the centre, knocking into one of the ladies eating a chocolate fudge sundae. She fell forward face-first into the dessert and came up with cream and chocolate dripping from her nose. Her husband went mad and punched him straight on the nose, knocking him onto another table (thank God it was empty). I rushed over and got him out of the restaurant quickly and sat him down to stop him from falling over.

I then rushed into the restaurant to calm everyone down, which soon happened, and I bought a round of drinks for the round table, who were soon laughing it off. The three left sitting on our corner table were very quiet. I told them not to worry and I was sure they would laugh about it the next day. They were apologising when we noticed his friend outside had come back in. I rushed over to stop him. He just said, "I want my coat and my wife, and we are leaving. Tell them we are going home and not staying at their house," which I did. 'Them' referred to his now ex-friends. We never saw our regular customers again.

Chapter 14 - The Naked Diner (no pictures included)

This chapter is nothing to do with Jamie Oliver, who got nicknamed the 'Naked Chef' for his revolutionary ideas and approach to cooking (he certainly introduced a more fun approach to cooking, but never appeared naked in his famous television shows). This is about a few of our diners who suddenly decided, or on impulse, to reveal parts of themselves that they would probably never show in public.

This sort of behaviour became popular in the 80s and was often seen at sporting events when a spectator would run across the playing field completely naked. This practice was known as streaking and often, I am told, would involve friends encouraging such activity.

I am not sure why exposing parts of one's body was such fun in the Palm Suite, and it could happen at any time with male or female diners.

As a keen photographer, I would take pictures of our customers in the restaurant. Large parties, often hen parties, were always keen to have photos taken and it wasn't uncommon just before the camera flashed that someone would lift her blouse to show off her breasts. I often didn't notice anything until I had the pictures developed, to my shock. I know this was done as a joke, often under the influence of drink, but thought it best not to show such scenes to returning diners. The far less attractive picture was a gentleman's bottom which was known as mooning!

Music was a large part of the restaurant and, as the evening gained pace and the food had been served, a dance to finish the evening off was quite common. The drinks would continue to flow and, on occasions, they would be dancing on the tables, which, over the years, has been a popular activity in restaurants. I have even witnessed items of ladies' clothing being thrown around the room, as they impersonated a striptease. I remember my surprise when one lady threw her blouse in the air and it got caught on our ceiling fan. I did stop the fan and return it to the embarrassed lady, who claimed, "I don't know what came over me." It did seem natural to some women while dancing on tables to combine this with removing their clothes.

The most outrageous was a loud party of Pinewood electricians and their wives, who managed to talk the birthday boy into doing a streak around the restaurant.

Fortunately, my efficient manageress got wind of the bet while serving them and trying to subdue their loudness. The birthday boy suddenly disappeared into the toilet and reappeared naked in the packed restaurant. My manageress was there with the right words:

"Surely, you're not wanting to show that in my restaurant." It worked as she pushed him back out of the restaurant. He reappeared fully dressed and very embarrassed.

If something outrageous is going to happen, you can guarantee it's going to be on a busy night when we are full. This Saturday night was no exception and I had a party of 6 couples on the round table and it was one of the chaps' birthday. His wife had asked me if she could have an acting policewoman who would come into the restaurant and want to arrest her husband for serious traffic offences. This sounded like a fun joke and so I decided to go along with it.

She asked me to meet the policewoman outside the restaurant and bring her in and point out her husband. This was a simple task which also gave me the opportunity to ask her what she was going to do. She told me she hoped to handcuff him and give him a good stripping down. I pointed out the chap and over she went, and he looked rather shocked. She read the offences out and asked for his hands behind his back, then quickly handcuffed him.

All good fun so far and certainly giving other customers a laugh. Then, she started to remove her jacket, loosening his shirt while singing a song. Then the police uniform was on the floor and the blouse was ripped off. Oh dear, how silly am I? This wasn't a singing telegram - it was a strip-a-gram! And then the bra was off!

"Quick, do something," I shouted at the barman and he passed me a tea towel, which I put in front of her breasts, which caused more laughter as she danced around. The barman came out to help with more tea towels so that she could dress. I told the table that it was not funny, so they laughed more but did apologise in the end, saying they did not know she was going to do that. By the way, she did undo the handcuffs.

Never again did I fall for that one and all such shows were banned.

Chapter 15 - The Iver Heath Locals

Local customers can often be the backbone of any restaurant, so we looked after our regulars well. As most of them walked to the restaurant, they certainly did enjoy a drink. We had one lady customer who used to call the restaurant her dining room, as she would eat more in the restaurant than at home.

The lady, whose name was Dorothy, was from New Zealand, and she lived in a flat opposite the restaurant. She had a regular man friend who used to meet her at the restaurant. We were never certain if they were married, but after a few years, they broke up. This then got even better for us, as she would meet her new boyfriends at the restaurant and they were out to impress, so they would always want to spend lots and pay. Dorothy often used to involve the staff and ask what they thought of him. Many a night, Dorothy would be the last one out of the restaurant, joining us for a nightcap and of course, we always made sure she walked back safely. They didn't seem to hang around long unless they got the thumbs up from us. This went on for a few years until she met a very nice chap called Malcolm.

They dated for many a year until they decided to tie the knot. This led to lots of 'getting married' parties, and to finish it off, the wedding reception was at the restaurant. We didn't often close the restaurant for an individual party, but this was one of our best and good fun for all, with some funny speeches including one from Dorothy which started off with, "Welcome to my dining room."

In the early years, the Palm Suite was very popular with dating couples, as it was still a relatively new thing to take your new girlfriend or boyfriend out for a meal, especially midweek (and we suited that trendy image at the right price). The Hard Rock Café opened 1971, Palm Suite in 1981, and we were one of the first hamburger restaurants outside of London.

I think the music we played also helped. Lively to start with, but come about 10:00 pm, we would slow it right down and get into the love ballads. The 50s and 60s were the most popular, which may have been why we often found ourselves still waiting to leave at midnight. We did have a tape that seemed very good at getting the couples to go home and my mother always played it if she was on late duty; it featured Perry Como. However, this was very popular with large drunken parties, as they would sing along. You can get rather thirsty after a good song or two. Next time you are looking up music, check out Perry Como. I think he's great and my favourite track is 'Caterina'.

As we became more and more popular with our regular couples, they started to propose and marriages started to happen. We even had a few proposals in the restaurant, especially on Valentine's night, when men were down on one knee with engagement rings. Great if they said yes, and most did.

While all of this was going on, my own marriage was not going too well, unbeknown to me. I had started to work longer and harder, which I needed to do as Julie and I had just moved from Marlow to Chalfont St Peter. This was a lot closer to the restaurant, so I was forever popping in to make sure they were okay. I never thought anything was wrong, as Julie was always busy in the house and as her parents only lived around the corner, they were always around helping us or she would go to see them. Or was she?

I had planned a trip to see some restaurants and catering suppliers in New Orleans with my brother and chef. We got cheap air tickets through my sister who worked for British Airways. Julie did not want to come and was gone on my return. Well, that was something I didn't have planned. Divorce happened quickly and then she married a friend of ours. That's life! So, life started again as a young, free and single restaurateur.

Adrian Getley was our first Pinewood film worker who rented a room from us. He was a talented guy who was involved in more complicated special effects, facial and body casting and customs.

The red devil costume you see in the next picture was made on the rear balcony above the Palm Suite restaurant. He decided to make it to his size, as he felt it would be easy to find someone for it to fit. He was not expecting to be the unknown star in the suit. This was for a sports shoe commercial that was being filmed on location in the Sahara Desert. Although filmed at night, this was very hot work stuck in a devil's suit as a goalkeeper, and he still didn't save the goal.

Adrian stayed in one of our rooms until he married, but his wedding reception was held in the restaurant as a farewell. He was a very nice guy who donated many of his facial castings to the restaurant, which I displayed in carefully constructed and lit glass-fronted boxes.

Over the years, Adrian made lots of memorabilia, from the facial casting of James Dean to the Wonka chocolate bar (this was just a plastic version, but they made 500 real chocolate bars).

Charlie and the Chocolate Factory
Release Date: Summer 2005

Chapter 16 - My Role as a Restaurateur

When I first got involved in restaurants, I never wanted to remain in the kitchen although it is the most important department in any restaurant. I decided to stay out the front and run the restaurant overall. This meant I could get involved in every department, helping with food ideas and writing new menus with my mother, and cocktails and wine lists with Sandy, the barman. I also helped with local advertising and promotion, wages and accounts which my father managed to fit in while running his printing company. In fact, he did most of it and just got me to sign the cheques and count out the wages. He was also good at curbing my spending on the restaurant as I was always looking at ways to improve and move us faster, but, of course, as he would say, don't bankrupt the business in the process.

The most important role I had in running the restaurant, and the one I liked the most, was the customer contact and attending to their needs. This is their night out so the atmosphere has to be right to start with, so music and lighting are very important. The music should not be at disco level but act as a barrier so you don't notice the next table's conversation. This can sometimes go wrong when a lively song finishes as it did for this poor chap who blurted out, "I don't want my mother-in-law staying this weekend". Others have been "of course I love you" and "I hate you" which did follow on by the lady pouring her large glass of wine over his head, and then walking out. I rushed over to him with some bar towels asking him what went wrong. He just said it was the wrong time and place to tell his wife about how good his new secretary is. It did turn out he was having an affair with her and we soon got to meet her. We later solved this problem by joining the music tracks up, but of course, this didn't matter when we got very busy later in the evening.

Lighting is very important - I was forever saying to the staff that I don't want the restaurant looking like a doctor's surgery. They used to think the lights were too low which maybe another reason why we were very popular with customers having affairs. So, being tucked out the way was having some benefits. We even had one customer who brought his girlfriend into the Palm Suite at lunchtime, and, when we opened our second restaurant, he would bring his wife there in the evenings. We had to be very careful not say anything but I nearly dropped him in it on his first evening visit by greeting him as if I knew him. I quickly covered up by being a very friendly manager and had to spend the rest of the evening being ultra friendly to all the customers, which some seemed to like and others found odd and funny.

If I came in after the staff, the lights would be adjusted down and probably the music changed to more lively tracks. Sometimes the waitress would get a complaint from a customer that he felt he had been plunged into darkness, and all of a sudden, the music was too loud. They soon got used to it as they never left quickly and may have stayed longer.

We have the atmosphere and lighting right, so next thing, check the waiting staff, make sure they are in good moods and remind them the diners do not come here to see us, they come for what we have to offer and, most importantly, the food and drink. As waiting staff, we can enhance the enjoyment of their evening by being efficient and correct with taking the orders. A wrong order can turn into a big cock-up, so always check what you give the chef because that is what he will cook, right or wrong. I have had chefs go mad at the waiting staff over a wrong order. I am then calming him down to re-cook a meal as fast as he can and apologising to the customer with normally means drinks on the house.

If you get bogged down in conversation with a diner and need rescuing, I or one of my colleagues must pop over and tell you the chef needs you. Then quickly, you go to the food hatch and say a few words to the chef. You are away and back to service. Don't go back to the table until its quieter in the restaurant. I had a waitress who got so bogged down with a chatting husband which angered the wife to point that Suddenly, she said in a loud voice, "If you carry on chatting to her all night, I'm going home!" This embarrassed the waitress and she ran out the back crying. A bit of an over-reaction but then I had to go out the back to calm here down. We switched the waitress off that table for the rest of the evening.

We always tried to have three waiting staff and two bar persons on busy nights plus a front-of-house manager. We also had four barmen, one full-time and three part-time. Again, they were all young men as that was what we could advertise for. Sandy was the full-time barman and our first manager and he helped me do the interviews and training. I think he did a good job at teaching the cocktails which was quite hard as we were still practising ourselves.

We always tried to have six waiting staff, mainly girls, in fact, all girls in the early days, as you could advertise for waitresses back then. One would be full-time and five part-time doing 2 evenings per week.

The training of the mixing of cocktails never seem to end; as soon as they got good, they seemed to leave. Of course, some never did get good especially the accident-prone ones who dropped glasses. bottles and knocked over drinks. We always used to tell them it was more important to make a good cocktail rather than throwing bottles around shaking them one-handed and acting flash. This reminds me of Simon who always wanted to shake the cocktail shaker one-handed. This one night, he was again shaking a Bloody Mary above his head when he lost his grip and loosed the drink over his head. The customers round the bar found this very funny as the red juice ran down his face onto his white shirt.

A favourite table in the corner for the film stars and regular diners.

Chapter 17 - Palm Suite Butchers

We became famous for serving great hamburgers, and it's a meal we never stopped cooking and improving. Our butcher in 1981 (recommended by John Ellner) was Larry & Kev's Meats from North London and they supplied our hamburgers, which tasted great. Larry & Kev decided to pack in the meat business a couple of years later, so we were onto butcher number two.

To find a good new butcher, the first thing we had to try was their hamburgers. This was something we involved the staff with, and a local butcher came up trumps as he made an excellent one. All his meat was top quality and some of it was from local farms. We did not make our own burgers back in the 80s and it wasn't until the mid-90s that we started to make them in-house.

In 1996, the British Health Secretary announced the dangers of mad cow disease, which led to 4.5 million cattle being destroyed. Our butcher only supplied us with Scotch beef so we had move to a butcher who could supply us with quality beef from another country. I found a butcher who could supply Australian beef and the quality was good (well, okay as it turned out). We put it on our blackboards that our beef was Australian, which the dinners liked.

As Scottish beef was given the all-clear and our new butcher did excellent Aberdeen Angus Scottish beef, we switched back, which pleased our customers. He also did a very good Scottish mince, mainly chuck steak with a small quantity of quality fat which is needed to make a hamburger. We then seasoned the beef and formed them into 6oz balls. Then, using a hand press, we would make our daily requirement. We stayed with this butcher for about 18 years until he decided to retire and sell his business for property development. Our account was placed with a new butcher who did not supply Scottish beef, so the hunt was on for a new one.

This was not an easy task as so many independent butchers had closed. We tried out four different butchers, all having problems with our requirements. Daily delivery was very important and my specifications on each cut of meat seemed a big problem. This was also now coming at a price for the restaurant as customers were voicing their concerns about quality.

We were getting near to Christmas and still had no regular butcher, when I came across Heanens at Roehampton, so I phoned and spoke to the owner, Shaun. He supplied top quality Scottish beef and made a special mince of chuck steak and brisket (single source and fully traceable) for us to make our Scotch beef hamburgers and cook them how the customers liked them. The customers soon realised we were back on track and we had a good Christmas. It doesn't matter how good your chefs are, if you give them poor quality produce, they will never serve a good meal.

I can recommend Heanen's Butchers for price and quality, so if you are local, definitely try them out. I am not local, but it's well worth the 20-mile journey to get there. Check them out if you can - you won't be disappointed.

Another visit to Heanen's Wholesale Meats at Roehampton, standing outside with Sean and David, the owners. Palm Suite's finest butchers.

HAMBURGERS

Hamburgers

Over the past fifteen to twenty years, it has become normal to eat a hamburger once or twice a week as a regular meal. The difference in quality that you can buy out is enormous. This could be from your hamburger van, often selling frozen ready-made hamburgers.

At the other end of the scale are fine dining restaurants that regularly like to feature a hamburger. These will often be made using rump steak, chuck, or a mix of single source beef. It is usual practice to ask the customer how they want it cooked, but a word of warning, this simple hamburger meal could cost you more than £20.

With all this in mind, why not start making burgers at home from scratch? If you do not have a mincing machine by now, and you like your hamburgers, there is no better investment. This can also be used to make a Bolognese sauce, chilli con carne, the infamous Greek moussaka and of course, many different types of meatballs. You can also mince chicken, lamb and pork.

I would like to explain how I think you can make great hamburgers in your kitchen at home. I do not think you can call hamburgers your own homemade recipe if you do not know what cut of meat was used. Supermarkets are very good at informing the customer where the minced meat has come from. However, I have never seen the cut of meat that was used to make the mince.

It is much better to use a local butcher who will be able to provide more information, including whether it's single source and traceable (which means it has come from one animal). Most independent butchers tell me they use 100% chuck steak in their mince. They also sell this diced which will save you a job cutting up the meat to go through your mincer. This is good but to make them yourself, you should start from scratch and buy the cuts of meat you want by weight, so you can keep a check on the quality and fat content.

I started off with an old hand mincer which was hard work and messy, and although worth the effort, it is much better to buy an electric mincer. I am very pleased with mine. It's safe and very quick to use which is great if you are having friends round for a summer BBQ or having a winter hamburger gourmet evening. Why not serve your very own hamburger at your next dinner party? Choosing the beef is important and most butchers will help you but look for good marbling and fat running through the meat. I think good chuck steak is the best cut and then, to change the flavour, a different cut of meat can be added. The very expensive cuts like fillet or sirloin don't work because they are too lean, but rump steak does.

Old-fashioned mincing machine — will improve your arm muscles!

Mincing machine in action, a time-saving must for every busy kitchen!

Modern electric mincing machine. Vine tomatoes, ready for your homemade ketchup.

I think there is more flavour and better texture if you blend 20/30% of another meat. Bavette, the French cut, works well, for example, but I do like brisket; it's cheaper and adds lots of flavour. I will list all the cuts I have tried, describing the flavours and the textures on the recipe pages.

1kg of meat makes 6 x 6oz burgers but a lot of people like them a bit larger for home-made. Don't worry about making too many as they keep well in the fridge using burger discs which seals the top and bottom. Some butchers sell these costing only a few pounds for a couple of hundred. At the Palm Suite, we used a hand press but they can't give is that authentic homemade look.

Before starting to shape the hamburger, it is necessary to season the meat, sometimes just with salt and pepper, and mix well. At the restaurant, we added the American seasoning called Old Bay. We also used one called Jonnie's which can be bought online but it is not cheap. You will soon find your favourite with the desired amount, remembering that seasoning is there to enhance the flavour of the meat, not mask it. I now have made two good seasonings which are mild to medium spicy flavour. These are a lot cheaper in the long run and you can store them in a sealed container which will keep them for a long time. Take a large handful of mince and form it into a ball, then onto the scales for the weight you want and repeat or copy the size. Then form them into the burger shape pressing hard enough so that the burger doesn't fall apart. Tap round the sides then place a burger disc on top so you can stack them. My chefs always used food handling gloves when making the burgers and I use them especially when mixing in seasoning or other ingredients.

There are a few different ways to cook hamburgers at home and the outdoor BBQ on burning coal is one of the best, but with no flames to prevent the hamburger becoming burnt.

Gas outdoor BBQs can also be good, as the English weather is not that predict- able, and a summer BBQ can be rained off on any summer's day, so you need a plan B. So back to the kitchen; if you do not own a grill pan, now is the time to get one. I invested in a large high ridged cast iron one that will last a lifetime so find the one you like but make sure it has high ridges for those BBQ markings. It takes about 8 to 10 minutes to heat a cast iron pan up, so make sure the pan you are using is hot.

Modern Cheese & Bacon Burger filled with tomatoes, lettuce and gherkins.

Don't put any oil in the grill pan as this will burn and burgers still stick. Instead, brush a little oil on the hamburger side to be cooked first and place into the pan listen for the sizzle.

I like my hamburger on the rare side so, as the beef I use is single source, I can safely cook them rare. We only used this type of beef at the Palm Suite. For rare, I wait till I see the blood starting to appear on the top of the burger before I turn it, then a couple minutes on the other side and let it rest on a warm plate. For my medium rare. I turn the burger again creating a cross pattern, and another quick turn for medium and so on if you want it done more. If you are not sure, you can do a small cut into the meat; this won't show with a topping or just in the bun. Steaks can be gauged by feeling the meat. The more you cook, the easier it gets but meat varies so much and it can often take longer to cook depending on the blood content. Well done ones are easy but may dry out with overcooking.

Homemade hamburgers from start to finish — but I don't have cows grazing in my back garden!

Beef hamburger meat

There are many different cuts of beef to choose from when making your hamburger, and these can really vary the flavour of the end result. Here's some of the different cuts of beef and differences between them. I would usually recommend a hamburger is made from chuck steak, and you can then mix in the other meats to add to the flavour. You *could* make a burger out of the other cuts though, if you really want to - I think the French like to do it that way!

Chuck Steak

Chuck steak will always make an excellent hamburger, as it has the right fat content of 15- 20%. The flavour is richly beefy with a tender moist texture. This cut comes from the large shoulder, however, it is important to say to the butcher that the meat is for making hamburgers, so he gives you a rich ruby-coloured cut of meat with some fat content. There are different sections of the shoulder and this cut is also very popular for slow-cooking.

Blending different cuts with chuck steak will help you get that great-tasting hamburger which you can call your own. I swap around all the time as I find they all taste good and it makes the task more enjoyable.

Rump

One of the most tender for mincing with good flavour but it is expensive. In my opinion, it does not make the best hamburger but it is very good as a 20% mix with chuck steak.

Onglet/Hanger Steak

A tender steak with a rich flavour as the cut is near the liver and kidneys. This gives the burger a distinctive gamy flavour. Mix about 15%-20% to chuck depending on taste. The French use this cut a lot for 'steak-frites'. It is called hanger steak because it hangs down from the tenderloin and rib.

Bavette/Flank

This cut is also popular in France served as a thin steak in many bistros. It has a very good flavour but can be a little coarse and chewy which makes it a very good cut to mince and add to the burger.

Brisket

The cut with a big hearty flavour. This is my favourite for blending and the one we always used at the Palm Suite. Again, this has the right fat content for flavour but do trim if needed making sure that any fat marbling is retained.

Short Rib of Beef also known as Jacob's Ladder

This is a fabulous, delicious cut of beef now seen on restaurant menus which has to be slow-cooked. This cut will give the hamburger a soft buttery texture. It is more expensive than chuck as you are paying for the bones. However, these can be used for stock, so wrap in cling film, label and freeze.

You can also use this cut to blend with chuck steak, as it will give you a good steak flavour to the burger. Short rib can have white fat on the top, so extra trimming might be needed to keep the right ratio of fat in the burger.

Skirt Steak/Cowboy Steak

A long cut of beef with a very intense beefy flavour. This tough cheaper steak will add great flavour to a hamburger with a 20% mix. Avoid this cut for cooking well-done hamburgers.

This is called the cowboy steak as the South American cowboys would put a piece under their saddle to tenderise it before cooking.

Flat Iron/Feather Blade Steak

This cut comes from the top of the shoulder area where the chuck is. It is full of flavour and is tender as long as the sinew is removed. This cut adds an extra beefy punch when added to the rest of the chuck when making hamburgers. The Flat Iron is also a very popular steak now and retains its tenderness when cooked rare to medium rare. This cut has become so popular that a small chain of restaurants named themselves 'Flat Iron'.

Hamburger Beef Mixtures

We always used Scotch beef in the restaurant for our steaks and hamburgers. This is not quite so important when making hamburgers but good quality beef will always give you a better burger. Look for a good rich dark red colour with fat marbling regardless of what country you are getting it from; you can get excellent quality beef sourced from anywhere in the world.

Below is a suggestion of different blends:

Chuck steak 80% Rump steak 20%
Chuck steak 85% Onglet 15%
Chuck Steak 80% Bavette 20%
Chuck Steak 75% Brisket 25% (Palm Suite Blend) Chuck steak 75% Short Rib 25%
Chuck Steak 80% Skirt 20%
Chuck Steak 80/85% Flat Iron 15/20%

Blending more than two different cuts of meat can get confusing as flavours will compete with each other and not complement or enhance flavour.

Method – Mixing (all percentages are approximate)

1 kilo of meat will make 6 burgers:

1. Cut beef into roughly 40 x 1 cm cubed pieces to go into the mincing machine. If blending, mix the meats together.
2. Mince the meat into a large container ready for seasoning.
3. Use choice of seasonings gently turning through the mince.
4. Split the mincemeat into required weight, normally 6oz/170g per burger.
5. Shape into a round ball distributing all the meat evenly.
6. If shaping by hand, press down on a flat surface edging around with your hands to form the hamburger shape. Turn regularly to get the correct shape all over and repeat if necessary, removing all cracks in the meat to make a firm burger ready for grilling. Burgers should be roughly 10cm diameter, 3cm thickness. If using a hamburger press, flatten to make the burger shape. Refrigerate until you are ready to cook; this holds the meat together.

At the Palm Suite, we used a manual hamburger press which worked very well for the number of hamburgers we cooked each day. These are available online as some people prefer to use this machine (a lot of butchers currently hand-press).

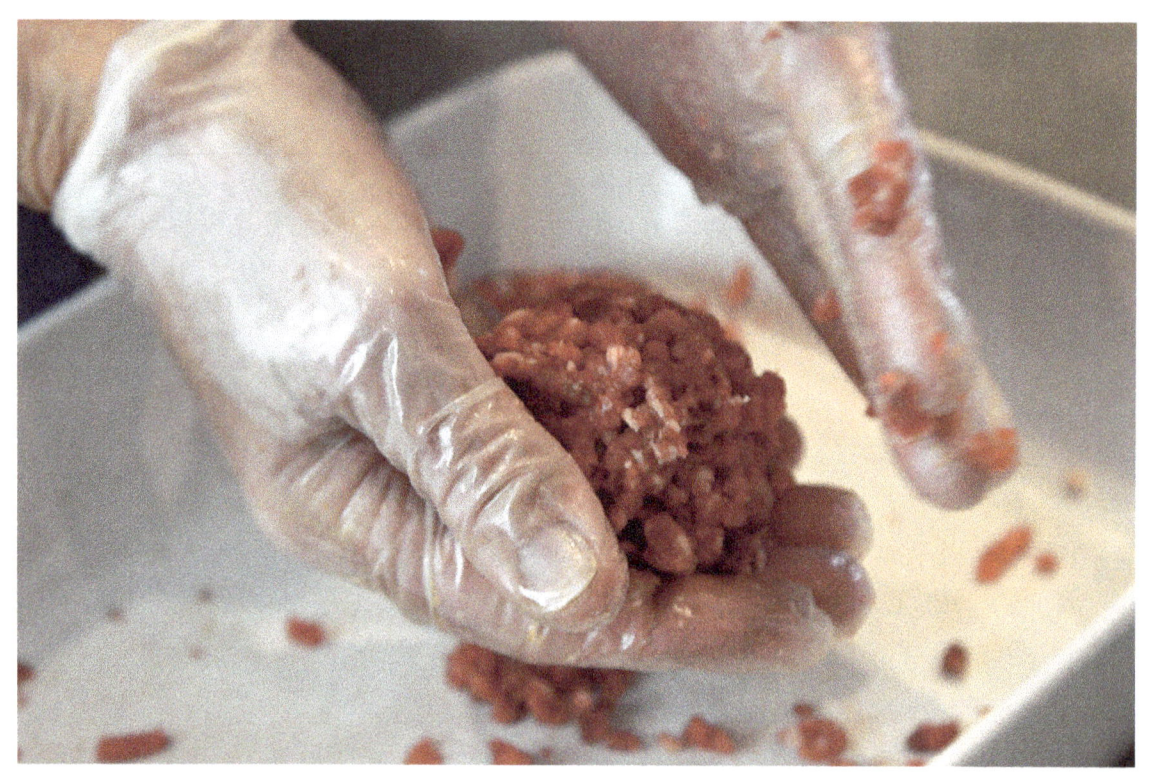

Making the 6oz rounds, ready to press.

Method – Cooking

1. Heat up your high-ridged grill pan (preferably cast iron) to a high temperature (approx. 5-10 mins*). Don't add any oil or fat to the pan as this will smoke the kitchen out.
2. Oil one side of your hamburger and place in the pan.
3. Leave approx. 3 mins* before turning. The edges of the burger start to brown and change colour.
4. Using a BBQ burger turner/spatula (metal if using a cast iron pan), the burger should come away leaving grill marks and a smoky aroma while cooking.
5. Turn over leaving to cook for 2 more mins* for a rare burger. The blood should start to rise to the surface.
6. For a medium burger, flip again rotating 90 degrees creating criss-cross marks on one side and leave to cook for another 2 mins*.
7. For a well-done burger, flip one more time and cook for two minutes*.
8. Once cooked, rest on the burger bun base while preparing the accompaniments.

*All times are approximate and will depend on the heat of the pan and the beef you have chosen for mincing.

Burger Buns

The original and still very popular hamburger bun is the sesame seed bun which can be warmed in the oven, toasted or placed in the grill pan to quickly warm through.

Other options include the newcomer to the burger scene - the brioche bun. This sweet bun blends nicely with the spicy seasoned beef.

We often use good quality light ciabatta rolls as an alternative to make a tasty change.

Sauces and toppings for Hamburgers

There are thousands of different toppings which can be put on hamburgers, and over the years at the restaurant, we certainly did many different sorts. Over the years, the old favourites always stayed, and we spent a lot of time perfecting them with top quality ingredients. We once named a hamburger after the very famous republican politician Caspar Weinberger back in 1987. This had a white wine and mushroom sauce in it. Not quite the same spelling but it was a jolly tasty hamburger as we know mushrooms are a great asset to any steak meal.

We did many different sauce toppings such as the crazy Shanghai hamburger, the Bombay hamburger with our delicious homemade curry sauce and the waistline hamburger (without the bun) that didn't do much damage for your waistline. There was the spicy peanut hamburger, the broncho hamburger, made with horseradish sauce, and the Hungry Horace hamburger that was 250g of meat. The hoisin hamburger was like the sauce in a duck pancake. Then there was the Rossini hamburger, the Texan hamburger, the BLT cheese hamburger, the Cajun hamburger and the 'fit and trim' hamburger.

For those of you who ate at Palm Suite and remember any of these and would like the recipe, do email me and I'll pass it on to you.

The Bacon Cheeseburger

This regularly came out as our best seller. This simple recipe relies on good quality mature cheddar with quality smoked back bacon.

2 slices smoked back bacon
50g mature cheddar

Method

1. Cook the bacon in the grill pan which helps oil the pan in preparation for cooking the hamburger.
2. Gently melt cheese in microwave without overheating and creating rubber texture which can split. (You will soon find your own favourite cheese for this process).
3. Place the bacon over the hamburger and pour over the melted cheese.

Blue Stilton and BBQ Sauce Burger

Stilton cheese and beef are a perfect combination in many different ways. With this recipe, we gently warm the crumbled Stilton to run into the warm BBQ sauce.

50g Stilton cheese
2 tablespoons of BBQ sauce (see BBQ sauce recipe below).

Method

1. Lightly warm Stilton in microwave or crumble Stilton straight onto the hot BBQ sauce.

Smokey BBQ Sauce

This is an excellent accompaniment for hamburgers, BBQ pork ribs and pulled pork sandwich. I have cooked many types of BBQ sauce over the years and this is a combination of many. I like to sometimes leave it chunky for hamburgers and blend for BBQ ribs, but both textures work well with many different styles of dishes. This tastes like a really good American sauce and does use a lot of ingredients. My sauce always does change a little bit but that adds to the joy of repetitive cooking. Add more smoked paprika if you like it smoky.

Ingredients

Olive Oil for cooking
2 red onions, finely chopped
1 tbsp fresh ginger, finely chopped
2-3 garlic cloves, finely chopped
450ml tin chopped tomatoes
250ml tomato ketchup
3 tbsp sweet chilli sauce
2 tbsp Worcestershire sauce

1 tbsp smoked paprika
1 tsp finely chopped fresh rosemary
2 tsp finely chopped fresh thyme
1 cup strong coffee (approx. 220ml)
1 tbsp smoked paprika
Honey to taste (approx. 2 tbsp)
Sugar to taste (approx. 1 tbsp)

Method

1. Lightly sweat off red onions, garlic and ginger in a pan over a medium heat for 5 minutes until softened.
2. Add the chopped tomatoes, tomato ketchup, sweet chilli sauce, Worcestershire sauce, fresh herbs, coffee and smoked paprika.
3. Bring to the boil then leave to gently simmer until the sauce thickens; about 30 minutes.
4. Stir in honey and sugar, and taste for the right sweetness.
5. Let the sauce cool then blend half for a chunky BBQ sauce or you can blend it all for a smooth texture.

Can be stored in refrigerator for several weeks.

Rob's Burger

If you're wondering who Rob is, he was my head chef for many years and probably the best, certainly the most consistent. He is also my younger brother who was in the printing business, but got a bit fed up with it. So, he joined the Palm Suite to fill a gap and wound up staying for eleven years.

Rob came up with many different toppings and flavours for our hamburgers and this one is one of my favourites. The accompaniment of his hand-cut coleslaw with the Palm Suite house fries made this meal a customer's favourite.

Try and buy the mince from a good local butcher, or better still, mince the beef yourself!

Ingredients (serves 4)

700g good quality minced beef (chuck steak or one of the recommended mixes).
Bag mixed lettuce leaves
1 large tomato or beef tomato
1 small yellow / orange pepper
1 red onion
8 small gherkins, sliced
200g mature cheddar cheese
4 Brioche buns
Salt and pepper to season
1 teaspoon Old Bay spice (or seasoning of your choice)

Method

1. Season the beef mince and form 4 equal balls, then flatten to shape into a burger.
2. Slice the gherkins, beef tomato, pepper and red onion into rounds.
3. Dice the cheese into 3 cm cubes, ready for melting in the microwave.
4. Halve the buns and warm in a low temperature oven (100 degrees 3-5 minutes).
5. Cook the burgers (method page 30).
6. Place the lettuce on the base of the bun and lay the burgers on top.
7. Top the burgers with the other ingredients and pour over the melted cheese (2 x 30 second blasts in the microwave).
8. Place on the plate a large spoonful of coleslaw with the Palm Suite house fries (recipe page 36).

Coleslaw

Our coleslaw was always very popular in the restaurant and a great accompaniment to any of our hamburger meals. We always used a good quality thick mayonnaise. We never made our own but have tasted some great homemade ones.

Ingredients (approx. 12 portions)

1/2 white cabbage
1 small onion
1 large carrot
200g thick mayonnaise
2 tbsp double cream
1 tbsp cider vinegar
1 tsp sugar
Salt & ground white pepper

Method

1. Finely slice the white cabbage and the onion together and place into a bowl.
2. Coarsely grate the carrot into the bowl and stir.
3. Stir in the rest of the ingredients and season with salt with pepper.
4. Store in a refrigerator until required; use within 4 days.

House Fries

These great chips came about due to the potato skins topped with cheese and bacon that we had on our menu. This American starter was a great seller but we were throwing away the potato insides. So we started to use these insides as our Palm Suite House Fries. These became so popular that we sometimes were throwing some of the potato skins away!

Ingredients (serves four)

6 large baking potatoes
Salt and pepper

Method

1. Bake the potatoes in an oven at 180 degrees, for about 45/60 minutes until just cooked.
2. Cool the potatoes then leave in the fridge overnight if possible. This stops the potato from breaking up.
3. Cut the potatoes into 4 or more, then cut away the outer skin leaving enough potato for potato skins if you are also making them.
4. Deep fry or shallow fry in an oiled frying pan turning to brown on all sides.
5. When the potato has turned a golden brown colour, season and serve.

They do hold well for 5-10 minutes in a hot oven allowing you to plate the burgers.

Ingredients to build the burger.

Lamb Burgers with Tomato and Red Pepper Relish

This is a great alternative to beef but it was always difficult to get our customers to try them. Once they did, they certainly liked them and soon became a blackboard favourite.

I like to use the leg as l think it makes better burgers than the shoulder. Of course, if you buy minced lamb in a supermarket, you won't have a clue what cut it is. So, invest in your mincing machine or ask your friendly butcher to mince some of his diced leg meat. These burgers benefit from additional flavours mixed in with the mince.

Ingredients (makes 6 burgers)

1kg minced leg lamb (not too much fat as they can taste greasy. 15/20%)

2 large shallots

1-2 garlic cloves

1tsp cumin

1tbsp thyme

1tsp spice seasoning (Old Bay)

2tbsp breadcrumbs or more if required to make the mixture firm

150g feta cheese

Tomato and Red Pepper Relish *(see next page)*

Method

1. Place your minced lamb into a mixing bowl.
2. Very finely chop the shallots and mix in with the minced meat.
3. Put garlic through a press into the mix.
4. Add the finely chopped thyme leaves and spices.
5. Stir in the breadcrumbs and form meat into burgers.
6. Heat up your grill pan and cook them for about 4-6 minutes each side turning once each side leaving grill lines. This should leave them slightly pink. They normally take a little longer to cook than beef.
7. Serve on a burger bun of your choice with Tomato and Red Pepper Relish, topped with crumbled feta cheese.

Tomato and Red Pepper Relish

This is a good, tasty relish that can go with many dishes including your Beef Burgers. This also keeps well in the fridge for 2/3 weeks in an airtight container.

Ingredients

1 large red onion
400g of good chopped tinned tomatoes
1 medium red pepper
1/2 red chilli pepper (med/hot)
2 tbsp red wine vinegar
1 tbsp tomato purée

1 tsp cumin
1/4 grated nutmeg
1 tsp sugar (if required)
Salt & ground black pepper
Olive oil for cooking

Method

1. Heat olive oil and sweat the red onion in a saucepan for 3-4 minutes.
2. Add red pepper and sweat for a further 2 minutes.
3. Add in the tinned tomatoes and red chilli pepper.
4. Stir in the rest of the ingredients and cook under a medium heat for a further 10-15 minutes, until thickened. Taste and add the sugar if required.
5. Add salt & black pepper to taste.

Chicken Burgers topped with Beetroot Relish and Goats Cheese

Today, in restaurants that serve a chicken burger, it is often a whole chicken breast in the bun. This is not a burger as I think you should always use seasoned minced meat. The beetroot relish and goats cheese work a treat with this recipe. We grow lots of beetroot at our allotment and always have some left over. Making this tasty relish goes with lots of dishes and keeps in the fridge for several weeks.

Ingredients (makes 4)

4 chicken breasts for mincing or 600g minced chicken

1 tsp rosemary, finely chopped (stalks removed)

2 tbsp fresh chives, finely chopped

Zest of 1 lemon

Salt and pepper

1 tsp mixed spice or Old Bay spice mix

1 egg, beaten

1 cup of breadcrumbs

Olive oil for cooking

Goats cheese (for topping)

Method

1. Mince the chicken breast using a large-hole mincing plate or use shop's mince. Place your mince in a mixing dish.
2. Stir in rosemary, chives, grated lemon zest, salt, pepper, spice mix and 1 beaten egg.
3. Form into hamburger shapes and coat with breadcrumbs.
4. Pan fry burgers in olive oil on a medium heat until cooked through.
5. To serve, top with beetroot relish and a couple of slices of goat's cheese per burger.

Beetroot Relish

Ingredients

3 large raw/cooked beetroots

1 tbsp capers

1 red onion

1 red chilli

3 vine tomatoes

Method

1. If using raw beetroot, place in the oven in foil with fresh thyme for 1 hour at 160 degrees.
2. Sweat off red onions and chilli for 2 mins. Add chopped capers and finely chopped beetroots.
3. Finely chop tomatoes and put through a food mill into the saucepan (alter- natively place the tomatoes in boiling water to remove skins, then de-seed tomatoes and add to mixture.) Stir into the pan until relish consistency. If too chunky, blend some of the mixture and return it to the pan.

Turkey Burger with a Beetroot & Apple Relish

This hamburger will convert any red meat loyalists with this jolly tasty alternative. I find that the breast meat makes the best burger, having tried the leg meat and other cuts. The onion and other ingredients help to keep it moist, so don't add too many breadcrumbs. The Beetroot & Apple Relish combination works well with the turkey. If you haven't bought your mincing machine yet, then you can get minced turkey in a lot of supermarkets if your butcher doesn't do it.

Ingredients (makes 4 burgers)

600g turkey breast meat for mincing
1 medium onion
1/2 garlic clove
1 small red chilli

1 tbsp fresh oregano
1 free range egg
1/2 cup breadcrumbs

Method

1. Mince your turkey breast meat and place into a mixing bowl.
2. Finely chop or quarter the onion and put it through the mincing machine, followed by a slice of bread which will push any remaining meat ingredients through the machine.
3. Crush the garlic and stir into the mixture with the finely chopped small chilli and oregano.
4. Beat the egg and stir into the mixture.
5. Add breadcrumbs until you have a consistency to form the burgers and refrigerate.
6. Cook the Turkey Burger in a grill pan, forming nice grill lines on each side. Once this is done, I like to pop it into the oven at 150°c for between 5-10 minutes so it cooks through. Turkey does take longer to cook than beef so if you are unsure, cut into the centre to check. Turkey can dry out so once cooked, serve on a warm bun and top with Beetroot & Apple Relish.

Beetroot and Apple Relish

This relish also goes well with chicken and will keep in the fridge for several weeks.

Ingredients

2 medium cooked beetroot
2 shallots
2 garlic cloves
4 tbsp of caster sugar

150ml red wine vinegar
1 crisp green apple
1 orange, zest and juice
1 tsp cumin

Method

1. Grate the beetroot and the apple into a medium saucepan.
2. Finely chop the shallots and add to the beetroot.
3. Crush the garlic into the mixture and add all the remaining ingredients.
4. Gently heat the relish, stirring until it's hot then simmer for 15 minutes.

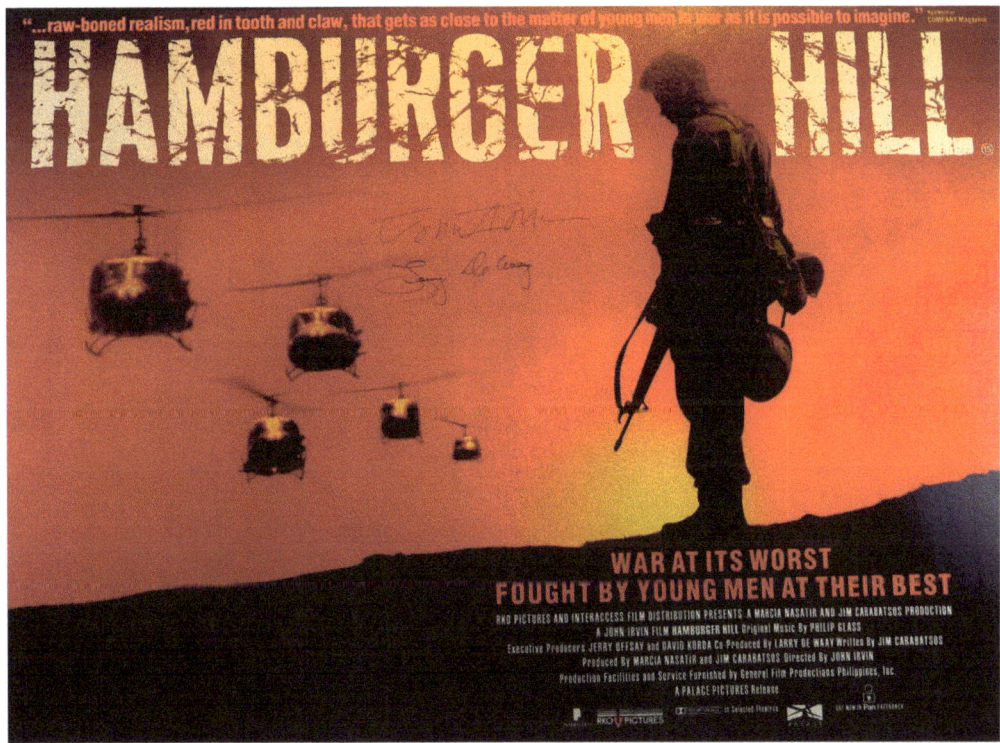

A signed poster of the film Hamburger Hill that featured in the restaurant - the film itself is not related to hamburgers but it was still pretty cool!

HOMEMADE STOCKS

There is nothing better than a homemade well-flavoured stock as a foundation for soups, gravies, stews and sauces, so stock what you're doing and get cooking...

Homemade stocks are cheap to make and should taste far superior to the expensive supermarket alternatives and will keep in the fridge for four to five days. Stock cubes should always be a 'no', especially as these often contain far more salt. If it is not possible to make stock, some of the stock pots are less salty than the cubes.

There is one that is endorsed by a famous chef and organic ones are available in supermarkets. Most people will not have the time to cook stocks on a weekly basis, so the best way to cook stock is in large batches which can be frozen in handy quantities ready for use later for that inspirational recipe. Having fresh stock available in the freezer can make all the difference and it's healthier too!

Good stock can be made from meat or poultry bones or vegetables, and gristle and trimmings can be added but not fat. Fish bones and trimmings make good fish stock to be used for sauces and fish soup.

It is not always easy to come by meat and poultry bones, but a good butcher will always have some. Veal bones do come at a premium these days and your butcher will charge a small amount but it's certainly well worth the cost as they contain the bone marrow for a good beef stock.

A good rainy day job – making your homemade stocks.

Getting fish bones is again difficult but if your town is still lucky enough to have a fishmonger, I'm sure they will be happy to supply you when you purchase the fish. A good investment is to buy a good stainless steel stock pot. These come in many different sizes, so I'd recommend buying the one which will be the right size for your use; as a guide, it will normally be larger than the average saucepan.

Beef/Veal Stock

When I was young, I hated the smell of some of the stocks my grandma and mother use to make. The beef is ok and my favourite to make but I still have the extraction on high to start with. As the roasted bones and the vegetables start to infuse the water and the aromas start to fill your kitchen, you will release why this will add so much to your dishes and beef stews.

Ingredients (makes about 1.5 litres)

1 1/2 kg veal or beef bones - Ask your butcher to cut the bones to 10-12cm pieces or small enough to fit in your pan

1 pig's trotter, split

1 carrot

2 onions (including the good brown skin)

2 celery sticks

Optional - A handful of dried mush- rooms

2 sprigs of thyme

2 sprigs of parsley

4 bay leaves

8 black peppercorns

1 tsp of salt

Method

1. In a hot oven, roast the bones at 180°c for 30 mins.
2. Heat a little oil in the stock pan and add the chopped vegetables stirring occasionally until golden brown.
3. Add the bones to the pot with the vegetables, then add the herbs and peppercorns. Cover the bones with water (roughly 5cm above the mixture) and add salt (the salt helps the scum rise to the top for skimming off).
4. Bring to the boil, then turn down to a low heat. Skim off the froth and scum, and simmer for 4-6 hours or until you are happy with the richness and flavour. Make sure the liquid does not evaporate below the bones, so if needed, add more water.
5. Let the stock cool for 10 mins before spooning out the large bones with a slotted spoon.
6. Sieve the stock into a bowl and reduce further if it needs to be more intense in flavour and thicker. When cool, refrigerate.
7. Leave in the fridge overnight then remove the solid fat from the top with a spoon.

Brown Chicken Stock

I always hear people saying chicken doesn't taste like it used to, and, in a lot of cases, I agree. Mass-produced chickens are not going to be as flavoursome as a free range bird or a corn fed chicken. For this reason alone, making good chicken stock will improve all chicken dishes, particularly the Sunday roast and stews.

Ingredients (makes about 1.5 litres)

1 whole cheap chicken (fresh or frozen)
½ kg chicken wings (optional)
2 onions (including the good brown skin)
1 celery stick (plus the feathery bits in the middle)
1 leek
1 carrot
2L water
8 peppercorns
1 teaspoon of salt
1 bouquet garni

Method

1. Roast the whole chicken and wings in an oven at 160°c until the juices run clear. Let the chicken cool, remove the breasts and cut the carcass to fit into your large saucepan.
2. Heat a little oil in the saucepan and add the chopped vegetables stirring occasionally until golden brown.
3. Add the chicken to the pot with the vegetables, then add the salt (the salt helps the scum rise to the top for skimming off) and peppercorns. Cover the chicken with water (roughly 5cm above the mixture).
4. Bring to the boil, then turn down to a low heat to simmer for roughly 2 ½ hours, skimming off the froth and scum. Make sure the liquid does not evaporate below the chicken, and if needed, add more water.
5. Let the stock cool for 10 mins before spooning out the chicken with a slotted spoon.
6. Sieve the stock into a bowl or container ready to go in the fridge when cool enough.
7. Leave in the fridge overnight, then remove the solid fat from the top with a spoon.

White Chicken Stock

This is a must for a lot of soups if you don't mind them not being vegetarian and it adds great flavour to your sauces. This is an easy one to make as you put all the ingredients in a large pan. Chicken wings do make a good stock, but other parts can be used, or cut up a cheap whole chicken.

Ingredients (makes about 1.5 litres)

- 2 kg chicken wings, raw
- 2 white onions
- 1 celery stick (plus the feathery bits in the middle)
- 1 leek
- 2 l water
- 1 bouquet garni
- 8 peppercorns
- 1 teaspoon of salt

Method

1. Put the raw chicken into the stock pot with the chopped vegetables, peppercorns and salt.
2. Cover with 2 litres of water and add bouquet garni.
3. Bring to the boil, then turn down to a low heat to simmer for roughly 2 ½ hours, skimming off the impurities. Make sure the liquid does not evaporate below the chicken, and if needed, add more water.
4. Let the stock cool for 10 mins before spooning out the chicken with a slotted spoon.
5. Reduce further if needed. Sieve the stock into a bowl or container ready to go in the fridge when cool enough.
6. Leave in the fridge overnight then remove the solid fat from the top with a spoon.

Fish Stock

Good fish stock is made from fresh, non-oily fish bones and head scraps of meat. Don't use salmon or mackerel, for example. This will add great flavour to soups and your favourite fish dishes. Keep for about 3-4 days in the fridge, but you can freeze to keep for longer. You can also make a shellfish stock by just using the shells or adding some to the fish stock.

Ingredients (makes about 1.5 litres)

1Kg white fish bones and trimmings (can be the head; don't use oily fish bones e.g. salmon, mackerel)
1 small fennel bulb
1 small white onion
1 celery stick
1 small leek

Half a glass of white wine (75ml)
1 clove
3 sprigs of parsley
6 white peppercorns
1/2 lemon (sliced)
2 bay leaves

Method

1. Sweat the vegetables in oil or butter until they are soft but not coloured.
2. Add the fish bones and trimmings, add the wine and heat for 2 minutes.
3. Cover with water, bring to the boil then skim off any froth or scum. Add the herbs, slices of lemon and white peppercorns and reduce the heat to a simmer for 20 minutes.
4. Sieve the stock into a bowl or container ready to go in the fridge/freezer when cool enough. Only store in the fridge for 2-3 days or freeze in small quantities for easy use.

Vegetable Stock

I don't think we give enough importance to vegetable stock. It's very quick to make and adds great flavour to soups and vegetarian dishes; it also freezes well. Don't use tomatoes or asparagus unless you are making that soup or dish.

Ingredients (makes about 1.5 litres)

- 2 carrots
- 1 parsnip
- 2 onions
- 1 fennel
- 1 leek
- 1 celery stick
- 1 garlic clove left whole
- 10 peppercorns
- 1 litre water or cover
- 4/5 sprigs thyme
- A small bunch of parsley
- 2 bay leaves

Method

1. Sweat vegetables in butter in a large pan until they start to soften.
2. Cover with water and simmer for 20 minutes, making sure the water does not evaporate below the vegetables.
3. Add the herbs and cook for a further 2-3 minutes.
4. Let the stock cool before using a slotted spoon to remove the vegetables.
5. Sieve the stock into a bowl, ready to use, or place into the fridge or freezer when cool.

Bowls and Small Plates

When we first opened, the most important thing about the starters was how quickly we could serve them. That doesn't mean to say they weren't tasty as the chefs would prep the hot ones so that they just required heating, and the cold would be prepared earlier and stored in the fridge.

So, having produced them in mighty quick fashion and with all running well cooking their main courses, or as the menu said then, "To Follow" which sounds daft now, we came across another problem... Our diners were spending too long eating some of the starters! The worst dish for this was a rather boring starter, Corn on the Cob, which we would heat in boiling water, add butter, black pepper and serve. It would take 5 minutes cooling before you could even consider biting it. Not a dish you would find on a menu today.

The next dilemma we had was what to call these introduction dishes, as restaurants use different titles that all mean the same. In the end, we decided to head our first menus "To Start" and "To Follow" - quite different at the time. We then went on to use the word "Appetizer" then "Starters", followed by "Bowls & Small Plates" which is my favourite title. The words we never used were Entrée or Hors d'oeuvres, which are French and sounded far too posh for the Palm Suite.

When I look back at the old menus we produced in the 80s, a lot of our starters were not very exciting and you wouldn't expect to see the Corn on the Cob on menus today. Prawn cocktail did make a comeback and Edna's homemade sauce was very good. We were very good at making soups, so I do hope you give some of them a go. Even better if you grow your own vegetables as we did in our allotment. The Chowders are rather different and a dish you don't see a lot of in England, so well worth cooking as a starter or main. Try cooking one; they taste really good.

Soups

Most restaurants have soups on their menus and Palm Suite was no different, serving a soup of the day. Most soups were made by Edna, and, in the early days, were always made with vegetable stocks suitable for vegetarians. We never did much for veggie customers in the early days, but our soups were always very good and Edna's homemade were the best.

Broccoli and Stilton Soup

This was one of our favourite soups with both the chefs and our customers. We always had a lot of Stilton in our fridge for our BBQ and Stilton hamburgers. The rich flavour of the Stilton certainly makes a very good soup.

Ingredients (serves 6)

1 kg broccoli

1 onion

2 sprigs of thyme

1 medium potato

1 litre of vegetable stock

1 tbsp lemon juice

A dash of Worcester sauce

A few drops of Tabasco (optional)

20g butter

15ml double cream

150g crumbled Stilton

Salt and pepper

Method

1. Chop the broccoli leaving the stalks in large pieces so they can be removed be- fore blending. Chop the onion; peel and chop the potato.
2. Sweat onions in butter for 4-5 minutes until soft. Then add the peeled and chopped potato, broccoli and vegetable stock.
3. Add the thyme leaves and Worcester sauce and simmer for 20 minutes.
4. Scoop out the large stalks and leave to cool for 10 minutes.
5. Blend until smooth, then pour back into the saucepan. Stir in the cream and lemon juice, then add the crumbled Stilton and Tabasco and cook for a further 3-5 minutes.
6. Serve immediately in warm soup bowls, seasoned as required.

Broccoli and Stilton Soup

Cream of Asparagus Soup

Cream of Asparagus Soup

This is one of my favourite vegetables and I am sure a British favourite as well, judging by the numbers of people at our local farms that do pick your own. This unusual-looking vegetable that spears its way up through the earth is well worth eating as fresh as possible.

I look forward each year to this short season which starts in April and finishes early June. As the season draws to the end, it is the perfect time to make asparagus soup.

Ingredients (serves 6)

1 onion, chopped
2 celery sticks plus feathery leaves
500g asparagus plus woody end bits
75ml dry sherry
1 litre of chicken stock or vegetable stock
150ml double cream
A small bunch of tarragon
20g butter
Salt and pepper

Method

1. Put the hard woody end bits of the asparagus into a small pan. Cover with water and heat until they soften. Strain and add the liquid ready to add to the soup.
2. Chop the onion and celery into small chunks and sweat in butter for about 5 to 7 minutes until the onions look translucent. Add sherry and stir for 1 minute; add stock and asparagus liquid, then bring to the boil.
3. Chop asparagus and add to the soup, then simmer for 15 minutes until the asparagus is soft.
4. Blend to a smooth velvety consistency and strain the soup through a sieve into another saucepan, pushing the liquid with the back of a ladle. Discard the remaining thick mush left in the strainer.
5. Warm the soup and add the cream and tarragon, stirring until nice and hot, then serve into bowls. Sprinkle a little chopped tarragon on each bowl and serve with crusty bread.

Cream of Mushroom Soup

Edna loved making mushroom soup and had many different recipes but this one was my favourite. Edna even found a local mushroom farm who would sell large boxes of them, either old or freshly picked depending on what she was cooking. Also, do look at Edna's Mushroom Sauce recipe for chicken which mushroom soup was the base for; it was a winner in the restaurant.

Ingredients (serves 6)

2 onions, chopped
1 leek, chopped
500g mushrooms, sliced
500g chestnut mushrooms
Sliced handful dried wild mushrooms
1/2 tsp grated nutmeg
2 tsp tarragon (optional)

Dash Worcester sauce
75ml cream sherry
1 litre of vegetable stock
2tbsp olive oil
20g butter
100ml double cream
Salt and pepper

Method

1. Soak dried wild mushrooms in boiled water in a bowl for 20 minutes before chopping the vegetables. (Do not discard the water).
2. Sweat onions and leeks in a large saucepan with butter and olive oil until soft and tender.
3. Slice all the mushrooms and add them to the pan with water and the sherry and stir for 2-3 minutes. Add a large dash of Worcester sauce with the mush- room water. Pour in one litre of fresh vegetable stock, stir and simmer for 20 minutes.
4. Let the soup cool, then blend all the ingredients, pouring it back into the pan for 2-3 minutes, while stirring in the grated nutmeg and cream.
5. Serve in bowls and sprinkle on finely chopped tarragon, with fresh crusty wholemeal bread. Season as required.

French Onion Soup

Cook this soup if your down in the dumps - you can have a good cry and blame the onions. When it's ready, this comforting dish won't fail to cheer you up! In the winter months, I think you can never cook too much of this soup. Try and use good home-made stocks as it will be well worth it for the end result. This recipe does not contain sugar, like many others, and it uses the traditional Gruyère cheese, which I think is by far the best with its nuttiness and caramel notes.

There are many different ways of doing the croutons. The tastiest is fried bread cooked in bacon fat or olive oil, but the healthier option is to just toast the bread.

Ingredients (serves 4)

6 large onions	2/3 thyme sprigs
2 garlic cloves	2tbsp olive oil
250ml French dry white wine	20g butter
75ml Brandy	200ml water to be added (as needed)
300ml beef stock	2 slices French baguette per serving
300ml chicken stock	40/50g Gruyère cheese per serving

Method

1. Peel and cut onions in half (from top to bottom), then slice into long thin strips. Peel and chop garlic.
2. Place in a large frying pan and fry until the onions become translucent and a light golden colour, then place in a roasting pan.
3. De-glaze the frying pan with the white wine and pour over the onions. Roast for 30 minutes at 160°c.
4. Place onions in a large saucepan and de-glaze the roasting tin with the brandy and add to the onions.
5. Pour in the stocks, add the sprigs of thyme (removing stalks) and bring to the boil, then simmer for 45 minutes. Add water if the soup starts getting thick.
6. To make the croutons, cut French baguette rounds (2 per portion) and fry in bacon fat or olive oil. Toast them if you don't want to fry.
7. Grate the cheese into a bowl ready to plate on the soup.
8. Pour hot soup into the bowls, place 2 croutons on top of the soup followed by the cheese on the top.
9. Place bowls under a hot grill to melt the cheese and remove with a cloth as soon as possible and serve. This can also be done by melting the cheese on the croutons, then placing them on the soup (this method is a lot safer).

Fresh Tomato Soup

We made this soup a lot during the summer months when vine tomatoes by the case were very affordable. They are often sold at fruit and vegetable market stalls or your local Asian grocery store. If you have a Mouli/food mill you can make this soup very quickly as it removes the skins and pips leaving a rich, smooth tomato sauce for the soup.

Ingredients (serves 8)

- 1.5kg of vine tomatoes makes approx.
- 1 litre of tomato juice
- 2 white onions
- 1-2 cloves of garlic
- 1tbsp tomato purée
- 500ml vegetable stock
- 3 sprigs of chopped parsley
- 1tbsp brown sugar
- 2tbsp olive oil
- 2tbsp white wine vinegar
- 1-3 slices of brown bread (crusts removed)
- Dash of balsamic vinegar Dash of Worcester sauce Salt and pepper
- 100ml double cream (optional)

Method

1. Cut tomatoes in half top to bottom and place in a large saucepan with a little oil. Warm until the tomatoes begin to soften, pushing down with a wooden spoon. Place the lid on the pan, warming for 5-10 minutes until soft.
2. Remove the pan from the heat and place the food mill on top of a new saucepan and spoon out the soft tomatoes into the mill, turning to extract all the tomato juice and goodness, leaving the seeds, skins and the hard core on the top. (If you do not own a food mill, place the tomatoes in boiling water until the skins split. Then remove the tomatoes with a slotted spoon, skin, cut and de-seed.)
3. Finely chop the onions and garlic and sweat in a pan with oil until soft.
4. Add the tomato mixture, vegetable stock, brown sugar, balsamic vinegar, tomato purée and a dash of Worcester sauce, then simmer for 10 minutes.
5. Drop in the bread which will thicken the soup, then let it cool. This does sound unusual but it does work!
6. Blend all the ingredients thoroughly then pour it back into the pan. Reduce to the consistency required. Stir in the cream (optional) for an extra creamy flavour.
7. Season with salt and pepper, serving in warm bowls with a sprinkle of chopped parsley on top.

Food Mill or Mouli

This is really a very handy piece of kit to have in your kitchen and something you would find in most Italian kitchens. It purées cooked vegetables and soft fruit, so it is absolutely perfect for tomatoes. This does the job of removing the tomato skin, seeds and tough pulp, small enough to fit in a small cupboard or show it off and hang it on the wall.

Of course, you can remain frightfully British and put the tomatoes in boiling water and scald your fingers removing the skin and seeds. I have never seen them in British kitchen shops but you can, of course, get them on online shopping sites, and a lot cheaper than a food processor. Soups, sauces and purées; it does it all and saves time!

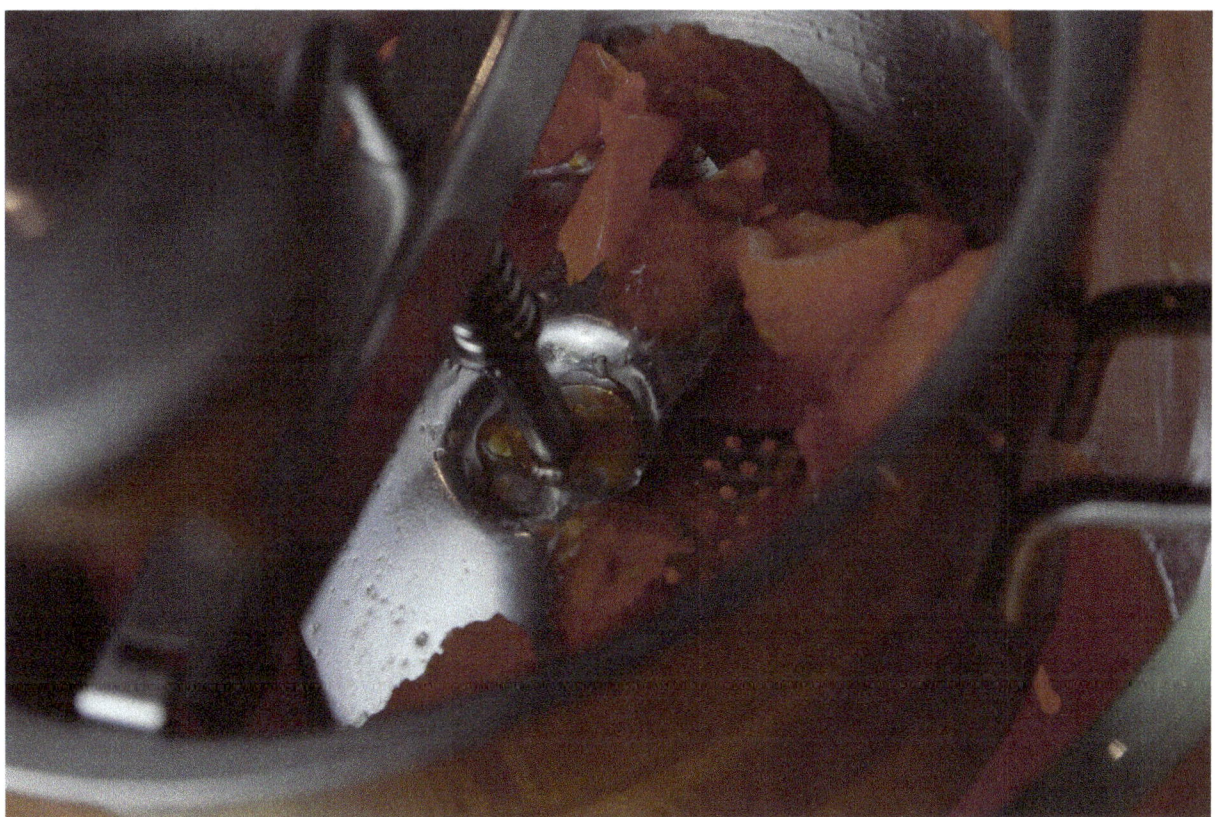

Tomato and Celery Soup with Goats Cheese croutons

Most years, we grow an abundance of celery at our allotment which makes an ideal summer accompaniment to the vine tomatoes.

Ingredients (serves 6)

1.5kg of vine tomatoes makes approx. 1 litre of tomato juice

250g fresh celery sticks

2 white onions

1-2 garlic cloves

1tbsp tomato purée

2tbsp olive oil

1 potato, peeled and cut into 8 cubes

500ml vegetable or chicken stock

1tsp paprika

1tbsp basil

Season with celery salt and pepper

Method

1. Cut tomatoes in half top to bottom and place in a large saucepan with a little oil. Warm until the tomatoes begin to soften, pushing down with a wooden spoon. Place the lid on the pan warming for 5-10 minutes until nice and soft.
2. Remove the pan from the heat and place the food mill on top of the saucepan and spoon out the soft tomatoes into the mill, turning to extract all the tomato juice and goodness, leaving the seeds, skins and the hard core on the top. (If you do not own a food mill, place the tomatoes in boiling water until the skins split. Then remove the tomatoes with a slotted spoon, skin, cut and de-seed.)
3. Chop onions, celery sticks and garlic, and sweat in the pan with a little olive oil until soft (not brown).
4. Add the tomato mixture and stir on a medium heat for a further 3 minutes.
5. Add the vegetable or chicken stock, potatoes, tomato purée and paprika, then leave to simmer for 20 minutes.
6. Allow the soup to cool and blend all the ingredients together. Then sieve the soup back into the saucepan, pushing down with a soup ladle to remove the stringy parts of the celery.
7. Season with celery salt and pepper, serving in warm bowls with goats cheese croutons (see next page) and chopped basil.

Goats Cheese Croutons

Ingredients (makes 6)

250ml soft goats cheese
6 slices of wholemeal baguette (or similar)

30g butter
3tbsp olive oil

Method

1. Cut bread into 6 circles, each roughly 2cm thick.
2. Fry in butter and oil until crispy.
3. Spread soft goats cheese on each circle.
4. Place in a medium-hot oven or under the grill for a few minutes to warm through the goats cheese.

To serve

1. Pour the hot soup into the bowls and carefully place large crouton in the centre of the soup.
2. Sprinkle with chopped basil.

Clam Chowder

This great American dish started to become popular in the 1700s and has been served in Boston at *Ye Olde Union Oyster House* since 1826. There are a few different types of chowders, but the New England and the Manhattan seem to be the most popular. A chowder is a type of soup or stew, so could be served as a starter or main course. This dish was introduced on our second menu, which we launched on 1st December 1981. This was not a good time to launch a new menu (unhappy chefs) but this soup was popular. When I cook this at home, I like to put the fresh clams in the steaming chowder in the last few minutes from cooking and then serve when the shells have opened.

Ingredients (serves 4 starters or 2 mains)

- 1kg fresh or frozen clams (fresh are expensive but worth it!)
- 6 slices smoked streaky bacon
- 2 onions, finely diced
- 1 Leek, split, washed and finely chopped
- 2 large potatoes, diced
- 500ml fish or shellfish stock
- 175ml white wine
- 300ml double cream
- 100ml water
- 4 drops of Tabasco (optional)
- 2 sprigs thyme
- 2 bay leaves
- 2 tbsp olive oil
- 25g butter
- Salt and pepper
- Chopped parsley to finish

Method

1. Fry the bacon in oil for a few minutes on each side, then chop ready to mix into the soup.
2. In a large saucepan, sweat onions and leek in butter and oil for about 5-7 minutes until translucent. Stir and keep the lid on or add a dash of water if it starts drying out.
3. Add the bacon and stir in the wine and bring to the boil, pour in the fish stock and bring back to the boil.
4. Dice the potatoes into 1-2 cm squares and add the potatoes, bay leaves, thyme and tabasco, then simmer for 10 minutes.

5. Add the cream and stir gently so as not to bash the potatoes, for a further 5 minutes until the potatoes are just cooked.
6. Add the clams and cook until the shells open. Serve in hot bowls and sprinkle with chopped parsley. As a main course, serve in large soup bowls with warm crusty bread.

If you are using cooked frozen clams, thaw well and add to the soup at the end for a few minutes; serve when they are hot. This still makes a tasty dish at a lower price.

Manhattan Clam Chowder

This soup first became popular at *Delmonico's Restaurant* in New York and is a tomato-based chowder, quite different to the white creamy New England version. I don't know which chowder I prefer, as both are equally as good.

Ingredients (serves 4 starters or 2 mains)

1kg bag fresh clams (or frozen)
6 slices smoked streaky bacon
2 onions, finely diced
1 leek, split and finely chopped
1 celery stick, finely chopped
2 large potatoes, diced 1-2cm
500ml fish or shellfish stock
400g tin of chopped tomatoes

150ml clamato juice or passata
100ml water (if required)
2 sprigs thyme
2 bay leaves
2 tbsp plain flour
2 tbsp olive oil
25g butter
Salt and pepper

Method

1. Fry bacon in oil and chop ready to mix in with the onions.
2. In a large saucepan, fry onions, leek and celery stick in olive oil and butter for about 5 minutes until they are translucent (add water if needed) and sieve in plain flour and stir.
3. Pour in the fish stock and bring to boil and add the diced potatoes, thyme and bay leaves, then simmer for 10 minutes.
4. Pour in the clamato juice (or passata) and chopped tomatoes, then simmer for a further 10 minutes or until the potatoes are cooked.
5. Time to add the clams and cook until the shells open.
6. Serve into hot bowls with warm crusty bread.

Chicken Satay

This is a very popular dish and there are many different versions. The very simple spice mix that coats the chicken is fairly standard. The peanut sauce we make is a lot more special and is well worth the effort. It transforms the dish to another level, while retaining some of the original flavours. I would advise you to wear rubber gloves while coating the chicken in spices unless you want your hands to look like you smoke 60 a day!

Ingredients (serves 8 starters or 4 mains):

- 4 chicken breasts (diced into roughly 3cm chunks)
- 12 wooden skewers
- 30g turmeric
- 20g cumin
- Salt & pepper
- Satay sauce (see next page)

Method

1. Combine the spices, salt and pepper and roll the chicken in the mix.
2. Skewer the chicken onto the sticks.
3. Heat up a grill pan (you shouldn't need oil as the chicken releases moisture but use if needed) and cook the chicken, turning when needed leaving nice grill marks on the chicken.
4. Place onto warm plates and pour on the sauce.

Satay sauce

This is a very good versatile recipe and will go very nicely with pork, chicken or beef. You can even top your burger with it! I use this on my chicken satay as I think it has more flavour than the traditional ones.

Ingredients (serves 6)

1 red onion, finely chopped
2 garlic cloves, chopped
2 hot chillis, chopped
1 lemon, (zest and juice)
20g palm sugar or golden caster sugar
3 kaffir lime leaves (finely chopped or zest of one lime)
1 tbsp olive oil
1 tbsp tamarind paste
150ml water
2 tsp rice vinegar
2 tbsp soy sauce ('Kikkoman' if possible)
340g crunchy peanut butter ('Skippy' if possible)

Method

1. Finely chop the red onion and garlic, then sweat in a pan with a little oil for 4-5 minutes.
2. Add the chillis, lemon zest and juice, sugar, lime leaves, tamarind paste and the water, then stir for 2 minutes on a low heat.
3. Next add the rice vinegar and soy sauce, continue stirring on a low heat.
4. Cool and blend the ingredients; return to the pan.
5. Finally, add the peanut butter, gently warming for a few minutes so it doesn't split. Add more water to your required consistency (if needed).

Mushrooms on Toast

This is a versatile dish that can really be eaten at any time of the day, from breakfast to supper. It is a good way to use up older mushrooms, but not too old as you will find the sauce mixture will go too dark. We put this dish on as a starter and it was very popular. In this version, I use baby button mushrooms and tarragon, which complement each other well.

Ingredients (serves 4)

400g baby button mushrooms
½ a small onion
25ml brandy (Spanish)
100ml chicken or vegetable stock
200ml double cream
2 tbsp olive oil
6-7 sprigs of tarragon
½ tsp of freshly grated nutmeg
Small bunch of chives
4 small slices of wholemeal bread

Method

1. Finely chop onion half and sweat in a saucepan with the olive oil for 3 to 4 minutes.
2. Cut the mushrooms into two or four, depending on size, and add to the pan. Cook for a further 3 to 4 minutes.
3. Pour in the brandy and flambé (this is creating a small burst of flames by lighting the Brandy, which adds to the flavour) or bring to boil.
4. Add the chicken stock and cook for a further 3 to 4 minutes, reducing the liquid. Then add the cream and stir.
5. Cook until the mixture starts to thicken and then add chopped tarragon leaves and grated nutmeg. Stir the mixture thoroughly.
6. Toast the bread and add butter if you want, then place the hot mixture on the toast. Sprinkle over fresh chives and serve. Garnish with chive flowers if you have any.

Buffalo Chicken Wings with Blue Cheese Dip

This is one of the most popular starter or snack dishes I have seen in America and features on thousands of restaurant menus. The dish was invented in New York and the chicken should taste hot. The blue cheese dips can vary a lot, as there are so many different types. I like to use fairly fresh, inexpensive blue cheese to blend with the mayonnaise and sour cream. An overripe cheese can spoil the sauce, so save your vintage Stilton for your cheese board.

Ingredients (serves 6)

2kg chicken wings/ drumsticks (or both)

Marinade

150ml chilli sauce, Tabasco or similar (do not use sweet chilli or oriental sauces)
1tbsp Worcestershire sauce
Salt and pepper

Blue Cheese Sauce

250ml mayonnaise
125ml sour cream
6cm of celery, finely chopped
3-4 drops of Tabasco

Dash of Worcestershire sauce
1 spring onion, finely chopped
75g of Stilton or creamy blue cheese

Method:

1. Marinade the chicken for 2 hours or overnight (the latter will be hotter and spicier).
2. Get a large roasting pan and lay the wings so they are not covering each other. Cover the pan with cling film and then tinfoil.
3. Heat the oven to 150°c. Then place chicken in the oven and turn down to 120°c, cooking for 2 hours.
4. Remove from the oven and allow to cool, then remove tinfoil and cling film carefully so you do not get a steam burn.
5. Remove fat and liquid with a large spoon. The chicken will be quite pale now, ready to be cooked on a higher heat. Place back in a hot oven around 175°c until crispy and golden brown.
6. To make the blue cheese sauce, mix all the ingredients together, taste and season. Keeps in the fridge for 2/3 days.
7. Serve on a plate with a small dish of the blue cheese sauce (not straight from the fridge).

Crab Cakes with Spicy Mayo

This is a favourite in American coastal towns, such as San Francisco, where fresh crabs are plentiful. Unfortunately, Iver Heath is not rich in such a product so we would buy a frozen 50/50 mix (white and brown meat). This is, of course, a lot cheaper but still makes a good crab cake. If you don't like the cheaper brown meat, use less or none at all, then just buy the white crab which is more expensive. If you are seeking perfection in your crab cake, buy fresh and drain well, removing any shell pieces.

Ingredients (serves 5-6 starters or 3-4 mains)

500g of cooked crab meat (fresh or frozen, white and brown mixed or just white meat)

½ a red, a green and a yellow pepper (the other half of each to be used as salad garnish)

1/2 red onion finely chopped

100ml mayonnaise

1 egg, whisked

50g plain flour

Small dash of Tabasco (just a hint of hotness is enough)

A large dash of Worcestershire sauce

Zest of 1 lemon

3 tbsp olive oil

100g breadcrumbs

Season with celery salt and white pepper

Spicy Mayonnaise (mix all ingredients together)

150g Mayonnaise

1-2 tsp Hot Chilli Sauce (taste for required hotness)

Season with Old Bay spice (or similar)

Salt and Pepper

1 tbsp of sherry vinegar

Method

1. Finely chop the onion and peppers and add into a large mixing bowl.
2. Whisk the egg and stir in the mixture with the mayonnaise.
3. Add the dash of Tabasco and Worcestershire sauce.
4. Grate the zest of lemon in the mix.
5. Stir in the breadcrumbs to make a firm mix.
6. Lastly, add the crab meat and fold into the mix leaving chunky pieces.
7. Form into cakes about 5cm and coat with flour.

To finish and serve

1. Shallow fry the crab cakes in olive oil until golden brown.
2. Place 2/3 crab cakes on a plate. Top with a teaspoon of spicy mayonnaise and serve with a garnish of mixed salad and a wedge of lemon.

Cheese & Bacon Skins

We had this dish on as a starter in the 80s and week after week it was our top seller. Yes! Not the healthiest of dishes but oh boy, does it taste good, and that's the problem with a lot of the food we love. If you eat it every day for the next 20 years, you may have some health issues but I wouldn't worry about the odd occasion. We did various topping with the skins and the Chilli Skins also sold well, smothered in Chilli con Carnie.

Ingredients (makes 4)

6 large baking potatoes
250g mature cheddar cheese
8 rashers back bacon
Salt and pepper

Method: Potato Skins

1. Oil a roasting pan and heat in the oven.
2. Brush the skins lightly with olive oil and season, then place in the heated pan and roast till golden brown.
3. While they are roasting, fry the bacon and cut into bite-size pieces.
4. Cut the cheese into 2cm squares and mix with the bacon.
5. Place potato skins onto a warm plate. Microwave the cheese in 2 x 30-second blasts stirring the cheese until smooth pouring consistency.
6. Pour off any oil from the cheese and then pour over the potato skins and serve.

One of our sharing platters in the 80s which we called Tangies & Tasties - only £3.95!

Appetizers

HOMEMADE SOUP OF THE DAY — 1·00

ORIENTAL WUN TUN. Petite parcels of pork wrapped in noodle dough, fried until crisp & topped with our own sweet & sour sauce. — 1·75

CHILLI SKINS. A cup of our famous chilli topped with cool sour cream & served with deep fried potato skins. — 1·80

DEEP FRIED CAMEMBERT. This famous French fromage is first breadcrumbed, deep fried & served with an apricot sauce plus apple slices. — 1·90

MELON & PRAWN COCKTAIL. Served with our own piquant sauce. — 1·95

PANCAKE ROLL. The Classic Chinese starter, with Szechwan pickled vegetables. — 1·50

DEEP FRIED CLAMS. A shellfish delicacy from the deep waters of America's East coast, strip cut, breadcrumbed & deep fried. — 2·40

CHICKEN SATAY. Tender morsels of chicken breast, rolled in herbs & spices, accompanied by our peanut sauce. — 1·95

HUMMUS. Nutty chick peas, tahina paste & a touch of garlic make this authentic Middle Eastern speciality very Moorish. Served with warm pitta bread. — 1·35

The starters we had on offer from our June 1986 menu.

Large Plates

This is a popular way of describing the main course in America and they certainly have large plates but with food piled on. The large plate idea also caught on in the UK, but with a lot less food and more stylishly presented. Some restaurant's plates were so large that they would hang over the table!

We used to have about 12 large plate dishes on our menu plus our blackboard specials, which changed all the time. The blackboard specials were very popular with our lunchtime Pinewood regulars and some of them would only order from it. I used to get very involved with finding and sourcing these dishes as they were so popular.

I would always bring back some very fresh fish when I took the family down to Littlehampton in Sussex, a very quaint coastal town stuck in the 60s, which had a wholesale and retail fish merchant on the river Arun estuary. It's next door to the Arun View Pub which is worth a visit. The children were not very keen on this holiday ritual, as they did not appreciate the smell of fresh fish, caught that morning, on our drive back.

They always had a good local selection of fish when in season and I would often buy the various sea breams, including gilt head and black bream. I always liked to get their plaice as the orange spots were always very bright, indicating good freshness. I was asked by a regular customer, John, if I could get some rock salmon and deep fry in batter like the fish and chip shops used to do. Now you would have to be at least my age to know what rock salmon was, as the trade's description officials stopped them using the name. The real name for the fish is 'dogfish' or 'huss'. Dogfish and chips doesn't really have much selling appeal. We sneaked rock salmon and chips up on the blackboard and sold loads.

This same regular, John, used to go game shooting and I asked if he could get us some fresh pheasants for the restaurant. Two days later, a dozen arrived at the back door and I was pleased they did. They had feathers, guts, the lot, and so I was soon to find out who the squeamish chefs were, as none of us, apart from my mother, had even plucked a chicken. Apparently, if we had asked, they plucked them for an extra £1 per bird. Back in the 80s, we all used to pop out the back of the restaurant for a cigarette where the pheasants were hanging, so I insisted the smokers had to pluck while they puffed. Of course, the staff renamed the cigarette break. We soon got through it and pheasant specials were up on the blackboard.

If you dined at Palm Suite and enjoyed eating our specials, you will find some of the recipes of the popular ones that sold well. Quality of the product was of paramount importance, sometimes not even making the right margins due to our low prices.

I won't go on about that as you will never believe me, but I do hope you cook some of them. As the French would say, "Bon appétit"!

Strip Cut Sirloin with Palm Suite's "Wild West" Steak Sauce

A very popular dish at the restaurant which very rarely left the menu. The marinade is very good and helps tenderise the meat. We used thinly sliced sirloin but it is an ideal dish for cheaper cuts such as hanger or flat iron. The dark rich sauce with fresh tamarind makes a perfect steak sauce. It keeps refrigerated for weeks so make a large batch. You will soon be dropping your favourite bottled sauces from your shopping list!

Ingredients (serves 6)

Marinade

- 3cm grated ginger
- 3 cloves garlic, crushed with the back of a knife and chopped
- ½ tsp ground black pepper
- 2 tbsp of pure maple syrup
- 2 tbsp rice vinegar
- 2 tbsp virgin olive oil
- Dash of sesame oil
- 2 tbsp light soy sauce (Kikkoman)

To make the marinade...

1. Mix all the ingredients together in a large bowl.
2. Place steaks in a large dish to take all 6 and pour over the ingredients.
3. Cover and refrigerate for 2 hours, or overnight, if possible, until you are ready to cook your steaks.

Sauce

- 1 large juicy mango
- 1 tbsp tamarind paste
- 75ml sweet soy sauce (Ketjap Manis)
- 1 tbsp brown sugar or more if you want it sweeter
- 3 tsp hot pepper sauce
- 250ml water
- 120ml tomato ketchup
- 2cm grated ginger
- ½ tsp paprika
- 1 clove of garlic, crushed
- Fresh ground pepper
- Celery salt

To make the sauce...

1. Peel and remove the stone of the mango and roughly chop.
2. Mix the rest of the ingredients together and blend.
3. Pour into a saucepan and simmer for 20 minutes.
4. When cool enough, pour into a blender and blend to a smooth purée.

To serve

1. Get a large cast iron grill pan (if possible), heat for several minutes until very hot.
2. Cook the steaks to the required level and place on the plates.
3. Warm the sauce through and pour over the steaks.
4. Serve with sauté potatoes or hand-cut chips and a watercress salad and seasonal vegetables.

Bearnaise Sauce

This has to be one of my favourite summer steak sauces if it's made right and to the right consistency. I have certainly tasted a few bad ones over the years. The taste of fresh English tarragon, preferably home-grown, is well worth the effort. This recipe never lets me down and when I got it right years ago, I wrote it down and stuck with it. Be patient when you start whisking; it takes a while.

Ingredients (serves 4)

2 egg yolks
¼ tsp or a pinch of cayenne pepper
2 tbsp white wine vinegar
125g good quality butter
20-25g fresh tarragon (home-grown if possible)

Method

1. Finely chop the tarragon leaves, discarding the stalks, and leave to one side.
2. Beat egg yolks with a whisk, then add cayenne pepper and vinegar.
3. Melt butter in a pan until it starts to bubble and remove from the heat.
4. Slowly add the egg yolks whisking all the time; whisk until your arm is falling off, and the mixture will start to thicken and can then be poured onto the steak.
5. Stir in tarragon leaves thoroughly.
6. Leave in a cool place ready to serve or remove from fridge 1 hour before serving.

Pork in a Madeira Sauce

This is an elegant, classy pork dish which has a friendly price tag. It is well worth sourcing good quality pork from your local butcher. This will enable you to serve it slightly pink and then more tender. Even if the pork is not your favourite meat, try this dish and it may convert you. I have converted a few over the years so why not give it a try?

Ingredients (serves 4)

2 whole pork fillets

Marinade

2 tbsp Dijon mustard
1 tbsp fresh thyme, finely chopped
Sea salt and black pepper

Sauce

2 tsp Dijon mustard
1 tsp fresh thyme, finely chopped
175ml Madeira
300ml double cream
Salt and pepper

Method

1. Trim up the outside of the fillet if your butcher hasn't done it.
2. Rub 2 tbsp of Dijon mustard, 1 tbsp thyme, salt and pepper all over the meat and marinate for about 2 hours or longer. Preheat oven to 160°c.
3. Lightly brown in a frying pan, then pop in the oven (you can put the pan in the oven or transfer to a roasting pan) for about 20 minutes.
4. Remove from the pan onto a chopping board and cut into roughly 3cm rounds.
5. Place the chopped-up fillets back into the hot pan, pour over madeira and carefully strike a match and light the spirit which will flame off the alcohol. When the flames die down, add cream, 2 tsp of Dijon mustard, 1 tsp thyme and heat for a couple of minutes.
6. Thicken sauce by further heating and then finish by pouring over the pork.
7. Serve with buttered mashed potato, or potato and vegetables of your choice.

Thai Poached Chicken Salad with Tahini Dressing

I didn't know what to call this dish but as a lot of the ingredients come from Thailand, that is how it got its name. I would have liked to have said I'd got this dish from a Bangkok back-street restaurant and the chef gave me his secret recipe but he didn't. In fact, I have never been to Thailand and I don't even know if they eat salad! Anyway, it's a jolly tasty, very different sort of salad, with a bit more work than the average, but worth the effort.

Ingredients (serves 4):

Poaching liquid

2 shallots
1 tbsp sesame oil
3 tbsp rice or white wine vinegar
200ml white wine
2 tbsp Ketjap Manis or dark soy
4 star anise

6 black peppercorns
1 tsp coriander powder
½ lemon zest and juice
1 hot red chilli, finely chopped
40cm piece of ginger (grated)

Method:

1. Finely slice shallots and place in a saucepan with a little sesame oil.
2. Add the wine, vinegar and Ketjap Manis and bring to the boil.
3. Add all the remaining ingredients and simmer for 10 minutes to infuse the flavours.
4. Carefully place the four chicken breasts in the liquid. Bring to the boil and then simmer for 15 minutes until the breasts are done. Test by cutting into the middle of the largest breast.
5. Cool and refrigerate until you are ready to serve.

Dressing

200ml coconut milk
1 tbsp tamarind paste / pulp
1 small red chilli, chopped
2 tbsp brown sugar
2 tbsp rice or white wine vinegar

2 tbsp Ketjap Manis
1 small garlic clove, chopped
20cm piece of ginger, peeled and finely chopped
75g Tahini paste from the jar

Method:

1. Add all the ingredients to the blender and blend for 3-4 minutes until smooth, then place in the fridge to cool.
2. This dressing will thicken in the fridge, so remove 5 minutes before serving and give a good stir.

Salad

Mixed salad (4 servings)
½ a red pepper, diced
½ a yellow pepper, diced
10cm cucumber, peeled and chopped
1 stick celery, finely chopped
2 spring onions or a bunch of chives, chopped
1 small bunch of Thai Basil, torn lightly

Method:

There are no rules with the salad, so add or remove what you like, but do keep the Thai Basil.

To serve

1. Place salad on four plates.
2. Slice the cold chicken breasts and place one on each salad.
3. Drizzle the dressing over the chicken. Place the remaining dressing in a serving jug for extra.

Pork Belly

This is one of my favourite meals and although it becomes a labour of love, it's well worth it. At Palm Suite, we had it on the menu for years served on champ. It's cooked in two stages, so the first stage will keep in the fridge for 4-5 days or in the freezer in wrapped portions.

Ingredients (serves 6 large portions)

3kg good quality pork belly
2 large onions, chopped
2 large carrots, chopped
2 celery sticks, chopped
1 fennel, chopped
10 black peppercorns
5-6 star anise

1 tsp chilli flakes
2 bay leaves
1 large garlic clove, diced
4-inch sprig of rosemary
2 sprigs of thyme
175 ml white wine
Water to cover

Roux

25g butter
2 tbsp oil
50g flour

Champ

1.5kg approx. of potatoes (preferably Maris Piper)
1 tbsp olive oil

2 tbsp cream
25g butter
2-3 spring onions

To serve:

Large round black pudding

Method:

1. Lay all vegetables, herbs, spices and white wine in the bottom of a deep roasting pan.
2. Place the pork belly skin side up over the vegetables and fill the roasting pan with cold water. Put cling foil over the pan then foil.
3. Cook in the oven on 140°c for 3 ½ hours. After 3 hours, take out of the oven to see if its cooked and tender. Open the foil and the cling film carefully so you don't scald yourself with the steam. Put a knife through the skin and if it goes through easily, it's done.
4. The belly should be soft and almost wobbly, so leave it in the tray until it is cool enough for you to lift it out onto a chopping board.
5. Cut the skin and about 1cm of fat away from the belly top and put to one side to make your crackling, leaving a thin layer of fat. On another flat surface, lay out 4 sheets of cling film, 6 inches larger than the widest part of the pork belly, overlapping each layer to make a longer strip. Roll the pork belly tightly into a cylinder. Do not roll the cling film inside the pork belly.
6. Once rolled, wrap the cling film around then twist and tie each end which will help give you a good shape. Place in the fridge for at least 3 hours or, better still, overnight.
7. Strain the cooking liquor and discard the vegetables from the pan. Pour the liquor into a saucepan and reduce by half, tasting for flavour. When cool, put the liquor in the fridge, allowing for the fat to rise for at least 3 hours.
8. Remove any fat from the pork liquor and transfer to a saucepan.
9. To make the roux, heat oil, add the butter and then sift in the flour; stir for 2-3 minutes to cook off the flour. Add gradually to the pork liquor to desired thick- ness.
10. Chop pork skin into roughly 2cm strips, then place in a roasting pan, covering with tinfoil. Heat in a hot oven for approx. 15 minutes until pork skin is crispy crackling.
11. Heat a frying pan to medium-hot and cut off the required amount of portions (4cm thick). Remove the outer cling film and place in the frying pan. Crisp both sides (roughly 3-4 minutes each side) for serving.
12. Fry the black pudding on both sides; it can be held in a 90°c oven until ready to serve.

Champ recipe

1. Boil good white potatoes (preferably Maris Piper).
2. Mash with butter, cream and a little virgin olive oil.
3. Finely chop 2 spring onions into rounds and stir through the piping hot mashed potato.

To serve:

Place champ at the centre of each plate, then place the pork belly on top of the mash, topped with the black pudding and crispy crackling. Serve with vegetables of your choice.

Rob's Lamb Stew with Spinach and Mint

This is a dish my brother used to put on as a special in those cold early Spring weeks. Rob would like to use a good quality shoulder, which has lots of flavour and is more reasonable than leg. I prefer to use the leg of lamb. Buy diced leg of lamb if your butcher does it. Both do a very tasty meal and I have been known to use both cuts. This should make about 6 portions depending on how large you want them.

Ingredients (serves 6)

100ml of cooking olive oil
1kg diced leg of lamb or
1 medium leg, diced
50g plain flour
2 large brown onions
2-3 medium size carrots
½ a litre of lamb or chicken stock

175ml glass of white wine 75ml sherry
1 tbsp Worcestershire sauce
1 tbsp chopped mint
250g spinach
2 tbsp chopped parsley
Extra water if required

Method:

1. Dust the cubed lamb with flour, salt and pepper.
2. Place oil in frying pan and brown the meat in small batches, then place in a large pot or casserole dish.
3. De-glaze the frying pan with sherry and stir into the meat.
4. In a saucepan, sweat off onions and carrots for about 10 minutes, then mix with the meat.
5. Heat the wine in the same saucepan and add to the meat.
6. Heat the lamb and/or chicken stock, then stir into the meat.
7. Add the Worcestershire sauce and give it a good stir. Add more water if required and stir in the remaining flour to thicken if needed.
8. Cook on the top of the stove on a low heat or at 150°c in the oven for 1 ½ hours.
9. When the meat is tender, turn the heat off and stir in the chopped mint and spinach.

To serve:

Pour into large warm bowls, sprinkle chopped parsley and serve with a bowl of buttered minted potatoes and crusty bread.

Jamaican Jerk Chicken with Banana and Papaya ketchup

This dish is sunshine on a plate and, of course, was a must-have on our Palm Suite menu. I employed many chefs from various Caribbean islands who did a wonderful job of cooking and presenting the dish. This version developed over the years so that it is not too hot and not like they would have it in Jamaica. This is easily remedied by adding your favourite finely chopped hot fresh chillies. Guava is also a great alternative to papaya.

Ingredients (serves 6)

Marinade for 6 chicken breasts

2 tbsp fresh rosemary
1 tbsp fresh or dried parsley
1 tbsp fresh or dried thyme
2 spring onions
3 tbsp hot pepper sauce
100ml of yellow mustard
Juice and zest of 1 lime
2 fresh oranges, juiced
1 tbsp white wine vinegar

Banana and Papaya Ketchup

1 onion
6 softened ripe spotty bananas
½ large papaya chopped (skin and seeds removed)
100g raisins
Juice of 2 oranges
Juice of 1 lime
1 tbsp white wine vinegar
1 ½ tbsp medium curry powder
1-2 tbsp brown sugar (if needed)

Marinade

1. Chop fresh herbs and spring onions.
2. Mix all the other ingredients together and add the fresh herbs and spring onions.
3. Marinade 6 chicken breasts in the fridge for 2 hours or overnight.

Banana Papaya ketchup

1. Finely chop 1 large onion and gently cook in a large saucepan until the onions are translucent.
2. Add 6 ripe chopped bananas and the papaya, then the raisins, and gently heat for 5 minutes, stirring the fruit.
3. Next, add the juice of 2 oranges, the juice of 1 lime and 1 tbsp of white wine vinegar. Then add 1 ½ tbsp curry power (mild or medium depending on taste).
4. Simmer for 20 minutes stirring regularly, then season with salt and pepper and sweeten with brown sugar if required.

To finish and serve:

1. Preheat oven to 160°c.
2. Remove chicken breasts from marinade and grill for 5 minutes either side and place in the oven for 10 minutes until cooked.
3. Place one chicken breast on each plate with 2 tbsp of the banana papaya ketchup.
4. Serve with rice, fried plantains or potatoes of your choice.

Fried Plantains

This banana-looking vegetable is a good accompaniment to a lot of Caribbean dishes. It does not taste like the fruit and has to be cooked. I like to portion half a plantain to each serving. These can be bought in any good Asian supermarket. They are larger than a banana with a thicker skin. I like to fry them in butter but you can also roast them.

Ingredients (serves 6)

3 large plantains
1 ½ lime
½ tsp salt
75g salted butter

They do look like overripe bananas but they are larger and firmer

Method

1. Peel the plantains like a banana and put in a large saucepan and fill with water, salt and the juice of a lime. Heat water to boiling and simmer for about 15 minutes or until a sharp knife goes through. Leave to cool and refrigerate.
2. When required, cut the plantain into quarters, then slice them lengthways so they don't look like bananas. They should be between 5-10mm thick.
3. Melt butter in a frying pan and fry the plantains on a low heat until they are golden brown and serve.

Making Tomato Juice for your Sauce

This is an essential sauce to keep in the fridge during the summer months when tomatoes are fresh and cheap. Fruit and vegetable market stalls or Asian stores will often sell cases of fresh tomatoes at a very reasonable price. If there is a choice, always get vine tomatoes as the smell and freshness is second to none and the drive home will make the trip down even the most boring road seem like you are driving past an Italian tomato field Mmmm, lovely!

Basic Fresh Tomato Sauce

1.5kg of Vine Tomatoes makes 1 litre of Tomato Sauce

Method

1. Slice the tomatoes from top to bottom.
2. Place the sliced tomatoes with a small drizzle of oil in a large pan over a low heat.
3. Squash tomatoes and place a lid on the pan.
4. Leave for a further 5 minutes before repeating squashing.
5. Leave for a further 5 minutes until tomatoes are soft.
6. Place 5-6 half tomatoes into a Food Mill/Mouli over a pan and extract juices, removing and discarding the unwanted pulp, skin and pips. Repeat until all tomatoes are juiced.
7. Place back in a saucepan and reduce to your required consistency. Store in the fridge or use.

Roasted Tomato Sauce

1.5kg of Vine Tomatoes makes 1 litre of Tomato Sauce

Method

1. Oil a roasting pan and place whole tomatoes with vines in the roasting pan.
2. Place in the oven at 160°c and roast for 1 hour, opening the oven after 20 minutes and prodding the tomatoes to reveal their juices. Repeat after a further 20 minutes.
3. Remove from the oven, let cool and discard green vines.
4. Place 5-6 half tomatoes into a Food Mill/Mouli and extract juices, removing and discarding the unwanted pulp, skin and pips. Repeat until all tomatoes are juiced.
5. Place in a saucepan and reduce to your required consistency. Store in the fridge or use.

Tinned Tomato Sauce

400g good quality tinned Tomatoes will make approx. 300ml of juice

Method

1. Place half the tinned tomatoes into your Food Mill/Mouli over a pan and sieve.
2. Repeat until all juices required are in the pan.
3. Reduce to your required consistency and store in the fridge or use.

Meatballs

Here is another good reason to have your own mincing machine. There are many different types of meatballs, using almost any type of meat including chicken and turkey, which you rarely see in supermarkets. Meatballs need less fat than hamburgers. They can be eaten with rice, potatoes, pasta, or cous-cous etc. We mainly did them as a blackboard special with pasta and fresh tomato sauce. They can be served as a starter or main course.

Aromatic Beef Meatballs with fresh Tomato Sauce

Try and use chuck steak again as the flavour goes so well with the other ingredients. You don't want to overcook them but most people like them done about medium and very easy to hold in a warm oven.

Ingredients (serves 4)

750g lean chuck steak / chuck mince	1 large egg, beaten
1tsp cumin	0.5 tsp chilli powder
1tsp coriander	100g breadcrumbs
1 teaspoon sumac	1 tbsp olive oil
2 large shallots, finely chopped	Season with salt and pepper
2tbsp basil leaves, chopped	

Method

1. Mince the chuck steak if you have a mincing machine. Place in a mixing bowl ready to add the other ingredients.
2. Put shallots through the mincing machine, which will push through any remaining meat followed by half a slice of bread, which will push through the remaining shallots, or finely chop shallots and add to mince.
3. Add the spices and herbs, sprinkling all over the meat, and gently mix in.
4. Beat one egg and mix into the meat then season with salt and pepper.
5. Add the breadcrumbs to get the right consistency, then roll them into 4cm balls.

6. Place the meatballs in a hot frying pan with 1tbsp olive oil and brown, turning when required. I like the meat to be on the pink side for more flavour.
7. Put into a roasting tin in the oven at a holding temperature of 95°c, de-glaze the pan with a splash of brandy (optional) and add juices to the roasting tin. Serve pasta on four plates, then place meatballs on top and finish with fresh tomato sauce (the tomato sauce can also be poured over the meatballs while still in the oven to keep hot).

Fresh Tomato Sauce Ingredients

500ml tomato juice (see page 165)
1 large red onion
2 garlic cloves
1tbsp tomato purée
200 ml tomato passata
1tbsp chopped basil

Method

1. Sweat onion and garlic in a pan until soft.
2. Add tomato juice and simmer for 15 minutes. Leave to cool and blend the ingredients if you require a smooth sauce (place back into the pan and heat, then stir in basil).
3. Add tomato purée and tomato passata and stir the sauce together.
4. Pour over meatballs (don't drip on the edge of the plate like photographed!).

Pork Meatballs

If you are looking for a cheap dish to feed the family, this is a good option. Pork is by far the cheapest meat, unfortunately for the British pig farmers who are going bust! So, before I start, I whip round for pig farmers (there are a few out there that are producing excellent pork). It does cost a little more, but well worth it for the taste. This type of pork is only really available from a butcher. Buy the cuts and mince your own. Another good reason to have a mincer! If you must buy pork mince from a supermarket, buy good quality, low fat.

Ingredients (serves 6)

500g pork neck or shoulder (if you have a mincing machine)

250g pork loin (or 750g good quality lean mince)

1 garlic clove, finely chopped

1 small onion, finely chopped

1 tbsp smoked paprika

1 tbsp chilli powder

1 tbsp cumin

1 tsp oregano

1 large egg, beaten

½ cup breadcrumbs

1 tbsp olive oil

Tomato sauce with basil

1 tbsp olive oil

1 red onion, finely chopped

2 garlic cloves, finely chopped

6 basil leaves

1 tin plum tomatoes

Grated parmesan

Method

1. Cut the pork into cubes, removing excess fat and sinew, then put it through the mincer (if you don't have a mincing machine, move to step 2).
2. Lightly sweat the onions and garlic in a pan for 5 minutes and let cool.
3. In a bowl, mix herbs and spices with one large egg and beat. Then add the onions and garlic and mix together.
4. Add breadcrumbs to the meat mixture until it is the right consistency for making the balls.
5. Roll the meat into balls and fry in olive oil until lightly brown and they are holding together.
6. Put it in the oven at 160°c for 10 minutes until cooked.
7. Serve in bowls over your chosen pasta and pour over the tomato sauce.

Tomato sauce with basil

1. In a saucepan, heat the oil and slowly cook chopped onion and garlic for 4-5 minutes.
2. Add tinned chopped tomatoes and stir, cooking for a further 10 minutes.
3. Chop the basil, then add half to the sauce.
4. Salt and pepper to taste. If you wanted the sauce smooth, blend.
5. Pour sauce over meatballs and top with the rest of the basil and grated parmesan.

Lamb Meatballs with Roquefort Sauce

This is another of my Greek recipes, which I had in the old port town of Naxos. Again, this is my own version of the dish. The creamy sauce with a hint of mint is a perfect accompaniment for lamb.

Ingredients (serves 4)

Meatballs:

1 kg leg of lamb diced or good quality minced lamb
1 tsp Old Bay spice mix (or your favourite!)
1 tsp Baharat spice (available at good supermarkets)
½ cup of breadcrumbs
1 onion

Roquefort Sauce:

150ml whipping cream
250ml full fat milk
75g Roquefort cheese
3 sprigs of chopped mint (plus extra for garnish)
White pepper

Roux:

1tbp olive oil
30g butter
30g flour

Method:

1. Mince 1kg of diced leg of lamb which you should be able to get from a butcher. If you don't have a mincer, buy good quality mince. Shoulder is also good if that is what your butcher uses.
2. After you have minced the lamb, put an onion through the mincer which pushes out the remaining meat and gives you a purée of onion.
3. Season with spice mix and Baharat spice, add about ½ cup of breadcrumbs and form into meatballs. Then chill the meat.

4. Make a roux with the oil, butter and flour. Cook through on a very low heat while stirring together. Remove roux from the saucepan into a separate dish.
5. Place milk and cream into the saucepan, heat and then whisk in spoonfuls of roux until you have a smooth thick sauce without burning. Crumble in Roquefort cheese until all the lumps disappear. Stir in the finely chopped mint (make sure to keep some chopped mint to sprinkle afterwards).
6. Salt and pepper to taste. Meatballs can be served with rice or pasta, placed in the middle. I also like it with sauté potatoes.

Barbecue Ribs

We first introduced BBQ Ribs to the menu in the mid '80s and they soon became a very popular dish. This was helped along with the opening of the Chicago Rib Shack in Knightsbridge that sat over 200 and still had queues outside for tables. The challenge was to get our pork ribs as tender, with a great tasting sauce.

This was done by cooking them in slow or holding ovens for several hours, or over-night. Then, we gave them a second-stage cook on our large American grill. This can be done at home on your outdoor BBQ grill or just finished off and browned in a hot oven. This is the reason restaurants have to do a second cook otherwise you would wait hours. BBQ also stands for 'Better Be Quick'.

At the restaurant, we used an American oven that also smoked the food. These were, and still are, very expensive ovens but certainly worth it for the Palm Suite. It had a separate compartment that you would put wood chips in with a hot element that would smoulder the hickory wood. This gave them a unique flavour.

Over the years, I have tried to simulate the Palm Suite ribs so I could cook them at home. This seems the right time to tell you how you can do it without spending a fortune on slow ovens. You are going to need a good local butcher to get these back or loin ribs, as they are rarely sold in supermarkets. You don't want the pre-cooked ones.

Allow one rack per person, ½ for a starter or ½ for a chicken & rib combo.

Ingredients (serves 4)

Serves 4

4 racks of pork loin ribs
1 litre barbecue sauce (see page 101)

Method

1. Use fresh ribs if possible or thaw frozen ones. Then remove the tough membrane on the back of the ribs, which will make the ribs more tender and will allow the sauce to flavour the meat on both sides.
2. Removing the plastic type of membrane is easy. Turn the ribs over so you are looking at the curve up and ease a knife between the meat and the membrane.

    Once you have lifted enough to grip, you will be able to remove it. This membrane does not soften with cooking so removal is well worth doing.

3. If you have made our chunky BBQ sauce, blend 500ml and liberally spread over the ribs, rubbing it in both sides. Leave to marinate for a stronger flavour in your fridge for 2 hours or up to overnight.
4. Place the BBQ ribs in large roasting tins, covering with cling film then tinfoil to really seal the cooking and make your ribs more tender.
5. Pre-heat oven to 160°c, place the ribs in the oven and then turn the oven down to 140°c. Leave cooking slowly for 2 hours. This will help tenderise the meat.
6. Remove ribs from the oven and uncover checking the level of tenderness. They should be cooked and slightly firm.
7. Uncover for 20 minutes in the oven to brown and serve; this can also be done the day after or up to four days if stored in fridge.
8. To serve the main course, place on a large oval plate and add potatoes of your choice and/or a mixed salad. Pour your homemade or favourite BBQ sauce over the meat.

Cajun Chicken Hotpot

This was a really popular dish which mainly featured on our blackboard specials. It was quick to make and my chefs used to knock up a large pot in about ¾ of an hour. Cajun cuisine is a style of cooking that came from France and then developed in the American state of Louisiana, the deep south. It can be quite spicy so follow my guide and taste the dish as you are cooking it for the flavour and hotness you like.

Ingredients (serves 4 - double to serve 8)

4 500g chicken breasts

5 slices of smoked lean streaky bacon

40g plain flour

15g Cajun spice (15g is mild heat, 20g is medium heat and 25g is hot, as a guide)

200ml chicken stock

300ml double cream

75ml medium or cream sherry

2 slim spring onions, finely chopped

1 fresh sweetcorn, kernels removed from husk (optional) or 200g tinned sweetcorn

Method

1. Cut up chicken breasts into cubes (3-4 cm), remove skin and bone if they are left on.
2. Mix 40g plain flour with 15g Cajun spice mix (or more if desired). Remember, more spice can be added when you have added all the ingredients together.
3. Roll the chicken in the spice mix. In a well-oiled hot frying pan, brown the chicken. Tip the chicken into a large saucepan.
4. Cut the bacon up into small pieces (2-3 cm) and fry in the same frying pan. Then tip into the saucepan with the chicken.
5. Pour away the bacon fat from the frying pan and de-glaze the pan with sherry. Bring to the boil and pour over the chicken.
6. Pour in chicken stock and heat on a low temperature for a few minutes. Then pour in the cream and stir the mixture, simmering for 15 minutes.
7. If you are using fresh sweetcorn, cook it before removing kernels and add to the pot.
8. Chop up two slim spring onions into rounds and add half to the thick creamy mixture.
9. To serve, place onto four plates with rice, sauté potatoes or fried plantains (see plantain recipe Page 163)

This dish goes well with your favourite American beer

Crispy Aromatic Duck Salad

Back in the 80s and 90s, every town in the south of England had 2 or 3 Chinese restaurants, which all seemed rather busy. We did a crispy duck salad without pancakes, which was very popular in the summer. We used to get asked for pancakes a lot, so I have also included a good recipe which I think is a lot tastier than the bought frozen ones.

Ingredients (serves 4 mains or 8 starters)

4 duck breasts

Duck Marinade

4 tbsp soy sauce 150ml sherry
1 cup of strong black tea (use 2 teabags)
2 tbsp olive oil
5-6 star anise
5-6 cloves
8 black peppercorns

For the salad

1 bag mixed salad leaves
1 bag of rocket or watercress (or both!)
½ cucumber julienne (thin strips 4mm)
4 small spring onions cut into thin strips
1 large carrot, grated

Plum sauce

100ml plum sauce
100ml hoisin sauce

Method

Steaming the duck breasts

1. Get a large saucepan and fill one third of water, then bring to the boil.
2. Place duck breasts in a large sieve, veg strainer or any other steaming device. Steam the duck breasts for about 20 minutes which will release the fat and keep your duck moist.
3. In a roasting pan, combine the marinade and mix together. Remove duck breasts from the steamer into the roasting pan and soak them in the marinade for about half an hour, turning regularly.
4. Cover the pan with cling film then tinfoil to get a nice seal. Place in a hot oven at 160°c, then straight away turn it down to 120°c for 2 hours.
5. Once the 2 hours have passed, remove the cling film and tinfoil and check the duck is cooked and tender.
6. We now need to crisp the skin, so turn the oven up to 175°c and place back in the oven for 10 minutes or until crispy.
7. Place salad on the plate with grated carrot and half the cucumber and spring onions.
8. Shred the warm crispy duck and place on the salad, then top with the remaining cucumber and spring onions.
9. Spoon over the plum sauce and serve.

Pancakes - Makes 10 6-inch / 15cm pancakes

75g plain flour

2 tbsp cornflour

120ml milk

1. Mix the pancake ingredients to a smooth, runny batter.
2. Heat a 15cm frying pan with a small amount of oil.
3. Pour in a small amount of pancake mix to cover the base.
4. Cook for about 2 minutes until the mix is going firm (try not to brown). Turn or flip the pancake over and cook for a further 1 minute. Don't worry if you mess the first pancake up; the second normally turns out well. Keep warm in the oven and repeat to the number required.
5. Spoon sauce on the pancake, place shredded duck, spring onions and cucumber in the centre, roll it up and enjoy!

Peppered Fillet Steak with Cream and Brandy Sauce

The English seem to have done many versions of this classic French dish, which is referred to as 'Steak au Poivre'. In France, it is common practice in up-market restaurants to make the sauce at the table. The steak would be seared in the kitchen and the head waiter would bring it out on his trolley. He would then prepare the sauce on a Calor gas stove in a brass frying pan. Then he would place the steak in the pan, pouring over the cognac and lighting it - flambé at its best. This theatrical display certainly does draw attention to this dish. We were never brave enough to do it at the table but the chef would light it in our visual kitchen.

I did discover that on occasions, the kitchen brandy used seemed a little excessive and possibly we were supplying the kitchen staff with the odd nightcap. The kitchen brandy was then put on the stock list. Thank heavens l was not using Cognac as they would in France.

The French traditional recipe would have French mustard but our Palm Suite recipe has Worcestershire sauce and a good squeeze of fresh lemon. Green pepper- corns are well worth getting as they are not as harsh as the black.

Ingredients (serves 4)

4 x 270g fillet steaks

2 tbsp olive oil

6 tbsp green peppercorns

2 tbsp brandy or Cognac 300ml double cream

2 tsp Worcestershire sauce

½ a lemon

Method

1. Lightly crush the peppercorns and lightly coat the steaks with them, pushing them into the meat on both sides.
2. Heat your grill pan up so it is nice and hot, then brush some olive oil on the cooking side of the steaks. Place in the pan and sear the meat on both sides; steaks should be rare at this stage but cook longer if required. Fillet steaks take longer to cook compared with other steaks, so if you are not familiar with this steak, make a small cut into one of them.

3. Transfer the steaks to a frying pan and continue cooking for about a minute, making sure the pan is hot. Now the tricky bit, pour the brandy/Cognac over the steaks and light it with a long match, standing clear of the pan as it ignites. If you don't want to do it that way, pour the brandy into the pan before the steaks, bring to the boil cooking the alcohol out and place steaks in the pan coating them with the brandy/Cognac.
4. Add the cream and stir into the brandy/Cognac and carry on cooking for a few more minutes, then turn the steaks.
5. Add the Worcestershire sauce and the lemon juice, stirring in.
6. Place steaks on warm plates leaving the sauce in the pan, then heat and reduce the liquid to a pouring consistency. Pour over the steaks.
7. Serve with your choice of potatoes and vegetables. Fried mushrooms and grilled tomatoes work well and green vegetables, i.e. any green beans.

This meal is a real treat and requires only a small amount of prep work before- hand. All fillet steaks are expensive and Scottish ones can be very expensive, but often have really good flavour.

Steak Kebabs in Oyster Sauce

This dish first appeared on our very first menu in 1981 and stayed around for many years. The sauce changed many times over the years and this one was one of our best. The oriental ingredients are available in most supermarkets these days. Easy to make and not a fresh oyster in sight, just a great flavour to add to your steak.

Ingredients (serves 4)

800g beef fillet or ask your butcher for trimmed fillet tail

4 shallots (echalion if possible)

1 red or orange pepper, de-seeded

Metal or bamboo skewers soaked in water (so they don't burn!)

Oyster Sauce:

3 tbsp Oyster sauce

1 tbsp soy sauce

½ tbsp sugar

2 tbsp rice wine vinegar

300ml double cream

300ml milk

Large dash Worcestershire sauce

Ground black pepper

Roux:

2 tbsp oil

25g butter

50g flour

Method:

1. Melt the butter with the oil then add the flour to make the roux. Cook slowly for about 4-5 minutes, thoroughly cooking the flour.
2. In a separate pan, combine the Oyster Sauce ingredients together, then simmer for 3 minutes.
3. Gradually whisk in spoonfuls of roux until your desired consistency.
4. Sweeten with sugar to taste and season if required. Add water to create a sauce consistency if needed.
5. To make the kebabs, cut steaks into 3cm cubes and cut up peppers (leaving 1 for later) and shallots to fit on the skewer. Place on the skewers: steak, pepper and shallots then repeat.

6. Heat grill pan or light BBQ. Rub a little oil over the steak kebabs and grill for 3-4 minutes each side for approximately rare or leave longer to your desired taste.
7. To serve, finely dice the leftover peppers. Place kebabs in the centre of plate, pour sauce over the kebab and serve the Palm Suite way with jacket potato and green salad, or the oriental way with rice or noodles. Scatter with diced peppers.

Grilled Chicken Breast with Ginger Mint Butter

This was the Palm Suite's winter dish for years, served on mashed potato with greens. It sounds an unusual combination with the mint and Dijon mustard, but it really does work. The ginger-mint butter melting over the chicken onto the greens and mashed potato finishes the dish off perfectly. Chervil is not an easy herb to get hold of fresh in the UK, so use dry or grow your own for future dishes. I often cooked this for the family at home and it turned into one of their favourites and a great recipe to get them to eat their greens.

My daughter Emily was very keen to use one of my restaurant dishes at her wedding and chose this one. One problem, though, was that the wedding date was in August, so I had to adapt it to a summer dish. This was easily done using crushed new potatoes and summer vegetables. See the pictures.

I will be surprised if this will not become a regular favourite dish, as it stayed on our menu for several years.

Choose from the winter version (top image) with balsamic greens and creamy mashed potato, or a summer dish with seasonal vegetables and crushed new potatoes (bottom image)

Ingredients (serves 6-8)

6-8 good quality chicken breasts

Marinade

125g Dijon mustard
2tbsp grated fresh ginger with juice
2tbsp dried chervil
125ml virgin olive oil
Fresh ground pepper

Mint butter

2tbsp fresh grated ginger with juice
125g butter (room temperature soft)
2 tbsp finely chopped mint (about 20 large leaves)

Mashed Potato

1kg good mashing potato (i.e. Maris Piper or Desirée)
50g butter
100ml double cream
Large dash virgin olive oil

Balsamic Greens

500g greens
3 shallots, finely chopped
250ml chicken stock
2tbsp Balsamic vinegar
25g butter
Salt & Pepper

Method

Marinade:

1. In a mixing bowl, stir grated ginger, chervil and juice into the Dijon mustard.
2. Then pour the olive oil and continue to stir; season with fresh pepper.
3. Trim and tidy chicken breasts if needed and coat them in the marinade.
4. Refrigerate for 2 hours or overnight.

Ginger mint butter:

1. Bring butter to room temperature so it is soft.
2. Grate ginger and finely chop mint and mix into the butter.
3. Place butter mix on two sheets of cling film and work it into a tube shape. Then roll the cling film around it so it's about a 3cm tube.
4. Place in the fridge for 1-2 hours so it's hard.

To finish and serve

1. Boil potatoes and mash with the double cream, butter and oil (salt and pepper to taste).
2. Place chicken breasts in a hot grill pan and mark both sides.
3. Remove from the pan and place in a hot oven at 160°c for 5 minutes, so the inside of the chicken is cooked.
4. Place two large serving spoons of hot mashed potato on a large plate. Then serve a large spoonful of warm greens next to the mash.
5. Serve the chicken last, topping with ginger-mint butter and enjoy.

If serving the summer option, simply crush your new potatoes with a large spoon or fork, with a large knob of butter and season well. Serve with summer vegetables of your choice, such as sprouting broccoli and baby carrots.

Crispy Lamb Salad with Mint Labneh

This is one of my favourite salads which I like in the winter or summer. In the winter, I tend to use the leftovers from our Lamb Sunday Roast. In the summer, I roast the whole leg the day before and store in the fridge overnight ready for the salad. Most large lamb legs will serve 6 people. There are no hard rules about which salad to use but this one works well. We also used to make a pork version of this.

Ingredients (serves 6)

2.5kg leg lamb
2 onions, chopped
3 garlic cloves, chopped
1 large carrot, chopped
1 stick celery
175ml white wine
1tsp chilli flakes
300ml chicken stock
Salt & pepper
2 tbsp olive oil

Salad:

Mixed lettuce leaves
(To cover 6 plates)
Half cucumber peeled and cut into chunks
24 cherry tomatoes, quartered
6 spring onions, julienne (3cm strips cut lengthways)
6 large radishes, sliced
1 pomegranate, seeds removed (wear apron)
6 dried ready-to-eat apricots
500ml plain Greek yoghurt
12 mint leaves

To cook the lamb

1. Sweat onions and 2 garlic cloves in some oil in a large frying pan for 3 minutes. Then add carrot and celery for a further 3 minutes until they are light brown. Be very careful not to burn onions or garlic. Place in a large casserole dish.
2. Trim off the outer fat and any sinews of the leg, place in a hot frying pan and turn using the end of the leg to brown as much as possible.
3. Place lamb in a roasting tin and pour over white wine, chicken stock and sea- son with salt and pepper.
4. Cover the lamb with tin foil and place in the oven at 150°c for 2 hours. Remove from oven and check to see if it is cooked to your desired level.
5. Cool and place in the fridge for a summer salad, or slice and serve with roast potatoes and winter vegetables.

To prepare the dish

1. Remove from the fridge 1 hour before you need it, then tear off bite-size chunks of lamb ready to fry.
2. Place olive oil in a frying pan, add 1-2 cloves of chopped garlic and fry for 2 minutes. Place lamb in frying pan with 1tsp of chilli flakes and fry till crispy.
3. Use your creative ability to create a salad mixture on each plate. (See ingredients).

Labneh

1. To make the Labneh, mix the Greek yoghurt with half a teaspoon of salt. Place the yoghurt in a muslin-covered sieve and put over a bowl in the fridge for 24 hours. This will show about 1 inch of liquid in the bowl. The mixture will get thicker the longer you leave it.
2. Finely chop 12 mint leaves and mix into the yoghurt.

To serve lamb salad

Place crispy meat on top of the salad and decorate with 2-3 spoonfuls of Mint Labneh.

Add some more mint leaves, a good dash of olive oil and scatter on the pomegranate seeds.

Fillet of Plaice on chunky pea purée with smoked bacon

You wouldn't think of placing bacon and fish together, but the combination really works well. I was certainly in the right *"plaice"* when I picked up this recipe for the pea purée. Enough of my plaice jokes, but I can tell you this was a favourite special with the customers. Always try and get good fresh large plaice, as small fillets don't really work and you only have to give one side per portion.

Ingredients (serves 4)

4 large plaice fillets (170g - 220g)
8 slices smoked streaky bacon
40g plain flour, seasoned
1 lemon, quartered
50g butter and a large dash of olive oil for frying

Pea Purée

4 slices of smoked streaky bacon
2 shallots, finely sliced
500g frozen garden peas or fresh in season
100ml water (from the cooked peas)
300g potatoes, peeled and diced
3 large sprigs mint
150ml double cream
60g butter
Salt and pepper

Method

To make the pea purée

1. Fry the sliced shallots with the bacon.
2. At the same time, boil the peas with 2 large sprigs of mint. Remove the mint and drain, reserving 100ml water.
3. Dice the potatoes then cook for roughly 10 - 15 minutes so they are still firm.
4. Add peas to the bacon and shallots and place into a blender or food processor.
5. Add the double cream and blend for 30 seconds, then add water to gain the right pouring consistency.
6. Put back in the pan and stir in the diced potato and season with salt and pepper.

To finish and serve

1. Dust the fillets in seasoned flour.
2. Fry 8 slices of bacon and keep warm.
3. Fry the plaice in a hot pan until light golden brown, about 2 minutes each side (slightly longer on the skin side).
4. Put about 4 heaped tbsp of hot pea purée on the centre of each plate and scatter with chopped mint.
5. Then put the fillet of plaice on the pea purée, add 2 slices of streaky bacon on the top, and lemon wedges on the side.

Palm Suite Fish Pie

Fish pie was always very popular in the restaurant and as we had fish delivered daily, our turnover was high. We would cut up whole fish, usually cod, haddock and salmon, removing skin and bones, but nowadays, you can buy fresh fish pie mix, smoked or unsmoked, even in supermarkets. Never use old poor quality fish; it's not worth all the effort of making the pies. If your town has a fishmonger, you will probably get a better fish mix and more varied. Good fresh fish will make a great pie.

Ingredients (serves 4)

750g fish pie mix (smoked or unsmoked)
250g raw king prawns, medium size (shells removed)
2 small leeks
2 garlic cloves
2 tbsp fresh tarragon
1 tbsp fresh parsley, plus some sprigs
1 lemon
300ml milk
300ml double cream
125ml Noilly Prat or white wine
Black pepper
Freshly grated parmesan cheese

Mash Potato

4 large Maris piper potatoes or similar
1 tbsp virgin olive oil
2 tbsp double cream
25g butter
Salt & pepper

Method

1. Check the fish for any stray bones and thaw prawns if frozen.
2. Place all the fish (not the prawns) into a saucepan and just cover with the milk, add a couple of sprigs of parsley and season with black pepper.
3. Heat the milk slowly cooking the fish for 2 minutes.
4. Add the Noilly Prat or white wine and the prawns, and cook for a further couple of minutes, till the prawns go pink and the fish is still chunky.
5. Strain through a fine sieve into another saucepan and put the fish into a bowl to cool, then remove the parsley.
6. Now make the sauce by heating the fish-flavoured milk and the cream. Simmer to thicken the sauce.
7. In a separate pan, heat oil and butter, then add flour to make a roux, stirring for about 5 minutes until the flour is cooked.
8. Add teaspoons of the above roux mix to the sauce, whisking until it starts to thicken and is a creamy pouring consistency. Stir in the tarragon and put to one side to cool.
9. Cut the leeks in half or quarters and finely chop. Crush the garlic with the side of the knife and finely chop.
10. In a frying pan, melt butter, add garlic and leeks and cook till they are starting to soften and just turning brown. Remove and cool.
11. Cook potatoes until soft and drain off water. Place back in hot saucepan, add the other ingredients and give a good vigorous mash until the potatoes are smooth. Then cool.

This can be all done in advance during the day and stored in the fridge ready to assemble.

To finish and serve

This can also be served in one large pie dish

1. Lightly mix the leeks with the fish.
2. Pour some sauce into the bottom of each dish and spoon the fish on top.
3. Season with salt and pepper, sprinkle on parsley and a good squeeze of lemon juice.
4. Then pour the sauce over the fish mixture.
5. Give the potatoes a good stir and spoon on top of each pie dish, running a fork up and down leaving lines and covering the fish.
6. Top each pie dish with some freshly grated Parmesan cheese. Place in a large roasting pan.
7. Put into a hot oven 175°c for about 20 minutes, the cheese should be going gold- en brown and the sauce bubbling on the edge. Push a skewer into the centre and it should come out hot to touch.
8. To serve, place a napkin on a plate and put on the hot pie dish on top, then you can carry it to the table. I serve separate warm plates so you can spoon on pie and help yourself to your choice of vegetables. Peas, broccoli and beans are all good.

Scottish Mussels in a Whisky Cream & Bacon Sauce

You don't have to like whisky to enjoy this dish. The combination of the cream and the smoky bacon makes it my favourite mussels dish. I first came across this recipe in a restaurant in Edinburgh, no surprises there, so this is the Palm Suite version. There is no need to buy an expensive bottle of whisky, so to keep the cost down, buy a small bottle.

Ingredients (serves 4 starters or 2 large main courses)

1kg Scottish mussels
1 medium onion
25g butter
Dash olive oil
3 rashers of smoked back bacon

50ml water
50ml Scotch whisky
400ml double cream
1 tsp thyme
2 finely chopped spring onions

Method

1. Clean the mussels in some cold water and de-beard them (this might look like hair outside the shell). Throw away any damaged mussels or ones that don't close after tapping.
2. In a large saucepan, sweat finely chopped onion in butter & oil. As they start to brown, add the water and lower the heat.
3. At the same time, in a frying pan, fry bacon to your chosen crispness. Drain fat off, chop and add to onions.
4. Bring cream to the boil, turn down heat and reduce to thicken so it coats the back of a spoon.
5. Turn up the heat and add the cleaned mussels.
6. Add the whisky (more if you want) and place a lid on the saucepan. Cook for a couple of minutes and they should start to open.
7. Pour in the hot cream and thyme and cook for a further 2 minutes until all the mussels have opened. Discard any that have remained closed.
8. Serve in warm large bowls with the whisky sauce and top with finely chopped spring onions.

Good Accompaniments:

Warm crusty bread and French fries — don't forget a large bowl for the shells.

Mussels in a Cider and Cream Sauce

Mussels have always been very popular in our restaurant. I always adopted my grandmother's and my mother's rule to only serve mussels with an 'R' in the month. In fact, we never found September or the last 2 weeks in April very good quality either. When very fresh, they will last a couple of days but never push your luck, as cooking quality is not about luck. They also won't improve your physical appearance! It's an easy meal to cook so eat them the same day; it's much better.

Ingredients (serves 2 large main portions or 4 starters)

1kg Mussels
3-4 medium shallots
½ celery stick, diced
1 tsp thyme
300ml dry cider (good quality)
400ml double cream
25g butter
Dash of olive oil
50g chopped parsley

Method

1. Clean mussels and discard any broken shells or any that don't close with a couple of taps (as these are dead). Remove the beards from the shell.
2. Bring cream to the boil and reduce to thicken.
3. While the cream is thickening, finely chop the shallots, then dice the celery into small ½ cm pieces.
4. Put shallots and celery mix into a large saucepan, add butter and a dash of oil, then sweat until soft and turning colour.
5. Add cider to the pan and bring to the boil, then add the mussels and seal the lid over a medium heat for a minute or more.
6. Pour in the hot cream and thyme and cook for a further couple of minutes or until all the mussels have opened.
7. Serve into heated bowls, discarding any mussels that have not opened. Pour over the hot cream sauce then top with chopped parsley.

Good Accompaniments:

Warm crusty bread and French fries — don't forget a large bowl for the shells.

Edna's Homemade Individual Steak & Kidney Pudding

This was so popular that our regulars would request it in the winter, then reserve one of Edna's amazing puds (I used to give the tipoff that Edna was making a batch!) Mother would normally make about 16 each time and they reheated well. I am going to cut it down to 8 but cook more if you want - they won't go to waste!

We had to adapt the steaming method which does work. You can buy the pudding basins easily online, so just look up 'Mason Cash' who are still one of the best — not expensive and it will last forever.

Ingredients (serves 8 individual dishes)

Suet Pastry

500g self-raising flour
250g shredded suet
Cold water (about 300ml)
Salt & pepper

The filling

1kg chuck steak
400g lambs kidneys
2 small onions, finely sliced
30g well-seasoned plain flour
1 tsp English mustard powder (more if you want)
1tbsp fresh thyme
Worcestershire sauce (3 drops per pudding)
Cold water

Covering the puddings with loosely topped tin foil to allow the puddings to rise

Method

1. Combine seasoned flour with shredded suet and slowly add the cold water, mixing together until you have smooth elastic dough. Lightly rub butter around each pudding bowl.
2. Leave for 5 minutes, then roll out the dough and place in the buttered individual pudding bowls and smooth out any cracks. Cut away any round the rim.
3. Add the leftover dough to the remaining dough for the lids.
4. Dice the steak into small cubes removing any sinew and save 5 cubes for making gravy.
5. Lambs kidneys have a core which needs removing. Cut around the centre core and dice into small chunks, then add to the steak. Keep the core for making the gravy.
6. Put seasoned flour into a bowl with thyme and mustard powder, then add the steak & kidney to the flour, coating the meat.
7. Place meat into pastry bowls with thinly sliced onions. Then add cold water so it nearly covers the meat, plus a few drops of Worcestershire sauce in each pudding bowl.
8. Roll out the pastry lids, dampen the edges and place on top of each bowl sealing well.
9. We now have to cover each pudding bowl with tin foil, so cut the foil with scissors to the right size. Then fold the foil in the middle creating room for the pudding to rise. It will only rise about 2cm.
10. Seal the edges of the foil round each pudding, (I like to tie each one with string) then put them in a deep roasting pan and pour water into the pan until it reaches halfway up the pudding.
11. Then cover the roasting pan with tin foil sealing all the edges well. Place in a hot oven at 170°c for 3 hours.
12. To make the gravy, place reserved beef, liver cores and onion trimming into a saucepan. Bring to the boil and simmer for a couple of hours, strain and keep warm.
13. Remove pan from oven and carefully take off the foil from the roasting pan and one off the pudding. Place a skewer through the top of the puddings to make sure the meat is tender. Ease a knife round the top of each pudding and turnover on serving plates. Gently remove each pudding basin.

Serve with potatoes of your choice and good fresh seasonal vegetables. I like buttered boiled potatoes, carrots and broccoli.

Sweet & Sour Chicken (or Pork)

In the eighties, when we first opened, men had long hair and wore tight shirts, open halfway down their chests. This has nothing to do with food, except they would like to swagger into the local, very popular Peking-style Chinese restaurants with their girlfriends. These restaurants were rammed every night and we also wanted some of the action! We started to copy some of the dishes but using fresh ingredients. The most important part of this dish is the sauce, which can accompany many different meats and fish.

Sweet and Sour sauce

Serves 6

- 1 red onion
- 1-2 garlic cloves
- ½ fresh pineapple
- 2-3 tangerines or clementines
- 250ml rice vinegar
- 8 tbsp golden caster sugar
- 50ml sweet chilli sauce
- 50ml tomato ketchup
- 3 tbsp cornflower mixed with water
- 2 carrots
- ½ yellow pepper

Method

1. Finely slice one red onion and garlic, then lightly fry in a pan for 3 minutes.
2. Cut pineapple in half, place down on a flat surface and remove skin. Then cut into quarters and remove the hard inner core. Cut each quarter into small triangles. Place in the saucepan and stir.
3. Finely grate zest of one tangerine or clementine and juice them. Add to the saucepan.
4. Add rice vinegar and caster sugar and start to gently heat.
5. Add sweet chilli sauce and tomato ketchup.
6. Add the peeled and grated carrot with the chopped pepper.
7. Add the cornflour mixed with 200ml water and stir to thicken. If it becomes too thick, add more water. Simmer on a low heat for 20 minutes.

Sweet and Sour Chicken Serves 6

900g chicken breasts (4-5 large breasts)

60g tempura flour or cornflour

½ tbsp of Five Spice powder

Method

1. Trim the chicken breasts and dice into 4cm cubes.
2. Mix tempura flour or cornflour with Five Spice powder, then dust the diced chicken. This gives the chicken a crisp coating when shallow frying.
3. Fry chicken in olive oil until brown and crisp.
4. Place on a plate and pour over sweet and sour sauce. Serve with rice and some soy sauce (Wok-fried vegetables are optional).

Sweet and Sour Pork

Serves 6

750g pork fillet

3cm fresh ginger

3 tbsp light soy sauce

1 medium size red chilli

Method

1. Peel and grate ginger into a bowl with juices.
2. Pour in the soy sauce and add finely chopped chilli.
3. Trim and slice pork, put in a large bowl and pour over the marinade. Then put in the fridge for 2 hours.
4. Fry the pork in a little oil for about 10 minutes until its cooked.
5. Place on a plate and pour over heated sweet and sour sauce. Serve with rice and stir fried vegetables.

Wiener Schnitzel (Veal in Breadcrumbs) with Capers and Lemon Butter

It will probably come as no surprise that this dish is the national dish of Austria, created in Vienna around the early 19th century. This cut of meat is not always available in supermarkets, so again, ask your friendly butcher for it and they will prepare it by bashing it out to a thin steak. This bashing out has a good tenderising effect on the steak. This version of coating the thin steaks with Dijon mustard I feel enhances the dish and the chilli flakes liven up the breadcrumbs. This dish also works well with a flattened chicken breast.

Ingredients (serves 4)

4 170g veal or chicken breast escalopes
2 tbsp Dijon Mustard
2 eggs
75g plain flour
120g breadcrumbs
2 tbsp Parmesan cheese

2 tsp fresh thyme
1 tsp chilli flakes (optional)
2 tbsp olive oil
75g butter
3 tbsp capers in white wine vinegar
1 lemon

Method

1. Lightly spread the Dijon mustard over the veal steaks using the back of a spoon.
2. Dredge the steaks in the plain flour.
3. Grate lemon zest over both sides. Remove skin from the lemon and cut into round slices to fry later with the capers.
4. Place steaks in the whisked eggs, coating them well.
5. Mix thyme, parmesan cheese and chilli flakes into the breadcrumbs. Then coat the veal/chicken steaks.
6. Heat olive oil in a large frying pan and place in veal/chicken steaks and fry on a low to medium heat. You will probably have to cook them in batches of 2 or use 2 frying pans. Turn them once they are a light golden colour.
7. Cook for a further minute and add the butter. When the butter has melted, add capers and lemon segments, then cook for a further minute until the second side has lightly browned.
8. Place schnitzel onto warm plates with potatoes. Stir the melted butter with the capers and spoon over the schnitzel.
9. Serve with a salad, or vegetables of your choice.

Edna's Vegetarian Nut Bake

This was our regular Christmas vegetarian dish which my mother used to make, probably why it tasted so good! Mother has now shown me how to cook this dish a couple of times and it's quite easy to get good, tasty results every time. I like to make more than I need as it freezes well and is a handy dish to have on standby for when your friends unexpectedly pop in, who still think Edna's cooked it.

Ingredients (serves 6)

200g cooked long grain rice (85g uncooked rice approx.)
75g white breadcrumbs
100g ground roasted mixed nuts
1 large onion, chopped
150g carrot, coarsely grated
200g chestnut mushrooms
1 tbsp fresh herbs (parsley, thyme, rosemary, for example)
200g mature cheddar cheese
285ml vegetable stock

Method

1. Cook the rice al dente, then leave to cool ready to mix with nuts and breadcrumbs.
2. Finely chop and sauté the onion, add coarsely grated carrot and sauté together for a further 2 minutes.
3. Stir in the finely chopped mushrooms and the herbs and pour in the vegetable stock.
4. Add the rice mixture, then spoon into a round baking tin.
5. Sprinkle with grated cheese and bake in oven at 150°c for 40 minutes. Once cooked, the top should be lightly brown in colour and firm to touch.

To serve

Place a portion onto a warm plate and serve with potatoes and vegetables of your choice. We used to serve it with roast potatoes at Christmas, but other times we would serve it with sweet potato mash and vegetables.

Cocktails at the Palm Suite

These amazing-coloured drinks were an instant success with our 1981 customers. The Palm Suite was certainly one of the first restaurants in the area to have a cocktail bar. Soon, there were more enough for the Buckingham Advertiser to do a survey on them. We were delighted when we won the newspaper's 'Best Cocktail Bar in Buckinghamshire'.

This was a fabulous bonus, although there was no awards to go with this extra fame, but the financial gains were enormous. The sales of cocktails would exceed over 200 on a Friday and Saturday nights. They were even popular at lunchtimes and our Pinewood Studio customers would often have one or two. I remember one chap drinking Blue Lagoons and as I was delivering his fourth, I said, "These are certainly slipping down a real treat". "Thank you, darling," he said in a loud voice. 'Darling' was a very popular word in the film business then but l have never been a darling before which left me feeling very embarrassed. This flamboyant character was in charge of a Wardrobe Dept on a film at Pinewood.

Recommending a cocktail drink to a customer in 1981 was not an easy task as very few people had ever tried one. We used to train the barmen to ask what spirits and liqueurs they liked, if they wanted a long refreshing one, (like a Mai Tai) or a stiff short strong one (the perfect way to describe a Martini). Maybe the wrong choice of words today but it was James Bond's favourite drink, and a lot of his jokes had a double meaning. However, Pierce Brosnan never ordered one when he dined with us.

In the early days, we only had cocktail barmen as that seemed to be who the customers preferred to make their drinks. We could advertise then for male or female positions. These sexist job vacancy adverts were stopped and it wasn't long before we had bargirls or bar women who were just as good as the guys.

Speed is an important part of making cocktails. A customer will soon get fed up if they have to wait a long time for a drink. Learning the ingredients was very important, so we created a cocktail sheet. This showed the glass, ingredients and the method of making the drink. A bartender must know the layout of the bar and where each spirit and liqueur is. You can lose so much time hunting for the Bourbon while making a Manhattan. A tidy bartender is essential, always placing every bottle back in the same place you found it straight away. Keep the bar clean having no sticky surfaces or hands. I don't want these sections to sound like a training manual but I hope these few tips will help you do cocktails at home for any sort of party, small or large.

Palm Suite Cocktails

BARBADOS COCKTAIL   3.00
For Two to Share.
Dark Rum, Light Rum Banana, Lime Juice, Sirop De Gomme, Pineapple Juice, Orange Juice

---

Old Favourites at 1.40

HARVEY WALLBANGER
Vodka, Galliano & Orange Juice

TEQUILA SUNRISE
Tequila, Grenadine & Orange Juice

MANHATTAN
Bourbon, Vermouth & Bitters

CARTERS COMFORT
Southern Comfort, Orgeat & Orange Juice

JOHN or TOM COLLINS
Vodka or Gin, Lemon Juice, Soda, Sirop de Gomme, Orange Juice

FREDDY FUDPUCKER
Tequila, Galliano & Orange Juice

MARGARITA
Tequila, Triple Sec, Lemon Juice

BLOODY MARY
Vodka, Tomato Juice, Lemon Juice, Tabasco, Celery Salt, Worcester Sauce

---

Specials at 1.70

MAI TAI
Dark Rum, Light Rum, Sugar, Lime, Orange Curacao, Orgeat, Grenadine

BLUE LAGOON
Blue Curacao, Tequila, Drambuie Tonic

SLOW COMFORTABLE SCREW
Sloe Gin, Southern Comfort, Vodka, Orange Juice

SINFUL SADIE
White Rum, Creme de Bananas, Orange Juice, Egg White, Grenadine

PINA COLADA
Coconut Cream, Light & Dark Rum, Pineapple Juice, Angostura Bitters

SCORPION
White Rum, Brandy, Orgeat, Orange & Lemon Juice

SINGAPORE GIN SLING
Gin, Cherry Brandy & Lemon Juice

DAIQUIRIS
Banana, Pineapple or Strawberry Liqueur, Fruit, Rum & Lemon Juice

---

Fizzes

CHAMPAGNE COCKTAIL   1.70
Brandy & Champagne

BUCKS FIZZ   1.40
Champagne & Orange Juice

Non-Alcoholic Cocktails

STEADY EDDIE	1.00
ST CLEMENTS	60p
MORNING SUN	60p

After Dinner Cocktails   1.40

BRANDY ALEXANDER
Brandy, Creme de Cacao, Cream, & Nutmeg

BANANA BANSHEE
Creme de Bananas, White Creme de Cacao & Cream

GRASSHOPPER
Creme de Menthe, White Creme de Cacao & Cream

COFFEE COCKTAIL
Coffee, Brandy, Cacao, Cream, Sirop de Gomme

CHAMPAGNE	10.00	CARLSBERG	60p
LIQUEURS	80p	SCHLITZ	75p
SPIRITS	70p	*WINES*	
		House *Red*	3.50
		House *White*	3.50
MIXERS	20p	By the glass	60p
		MUSCADET *White*	5.00
PURE ORANGE JUICE	45p	BEAUJOLAIS VILLAGES A.C. *Red*	5.00

Palm Suite's first cocktail menu, 1981

A cocktail menu we were extremely proud of, launched on 26th October, 1987

When introducing a speed to making cocktails, the accidents will increase and the more we rush, the worse they get. We certainly had had our fair share of accidents but it's the amusing ones I remember. The more colourful the drink, the more lethal they become if spilt over a diner. Unfortunately for the waiting staff, they were the victims of most spilt drinks. One Saturday night, a new waitress had taken an order for five cocktails. These were quickly made by the two bartenders and sat proudly on the tray for delivery. The waitress needed some help on which drink was which. The barman was a little annoyed at this request and was telling her quickly when his hand caught the tall reddish glass called the Mai Tai and knocked it over her. The mortified barman grabbed a tea towel and started to wipe her down. This made things worse as ice had gone everywhere and the cold red liquid was all down her white blouse. "That broke the ice between you," i said. My joke didn't go down too well but offering a new white blouse to change into went down a lot better. They did turn out good friends and often laugh about her first night.

This was not always the case when it came to customers which would often cost me money with dry cleaning, or worse still, a new garment. I soon found out the quickest way to recover from chucking drink over a customer was to buy the whole party a drink or a bottle of wine. Parties were always a problem serving drinks to as they tend to move around a lot and it's not easy to dodge around them. This would often be someone bumping into staff while delivering drinks. This, of course, would never be their fault so again, another quick round, and if it was all girls, this could be cocktails or champagne. Now the whole party is benefitting from the accident and they would smooth things over for me.

Ice aways plays an enormous part in a cocktail bar as you need so much of it and we could always run out on busy nights. This Saturday was no exception and required one of the barman running out the back to get more which should be done in a stainless steel bucket. This was slow as it would take several trips, so a large dustbin bag was preferred. This was fine until I bought a cheap batch that looked like good buy but had a tendency to split open

at the bottom. One Saturday night about 9.00 pm, the ice was getting low so out went the barman with one of our new large black bin bags and filled it with ice. As it was raining, he rushed back in swinging the dustbin bag through the restaurant as he rushed to the bar. The bag suddenly split and ice spilled out everywhere over the restaurant floor. The barman slipped onto the floor, falling on his back, sliding through the restaurant, right to the bar, where he came to an abrupt stop! The customers found this hilarious, thank goodness! We also just about had enough ice to make it through the night! Shortly after this event, he resigned. Maybe he never got over the embarrassment. I do have to thank him for giving us one of the funniest bar moments and excellent training on how not to bring ice through a restaurant.

The cocktails we served were starting to take off, particularly for the film crews and the celebrities. I'm proud that none of my staff ever divulged any details of their drinking habits to the press.

My first barman was a chap called Sandy, who soon mastered the art of making great cocktails. He became our first full-time barman and our first manager. He was very popular with our customers and staff, so much so that he married one of our waitresses! Sandy did leave us to open his own restaurant, then hotel. Enough about him; he can write his own book! The restaurant policy was not to encourage staff relationships. Despite this, at times, it felt like we were running a dating agency, rather than a restaurant! We did have a quite few marriages and divorces.

Trying to learn all the cocktails was never easy, so I encouraged the barmen to trust their memories and go for it. This was a good tactic until a customer from Jamaica was served a pink Pina Colada. I wanted to kill the barman; however, the customer drank it fairly quickly and promptly asked for another! Following a lively discussion between me and the barman, we agreed that the subsequent one should also be served pink. The customer commented that this was his first pink Pina Colada but it was ok and he said he would tell the folks back in Jamaica about our cocktails. If you have had a pink Pina Colada on holiday in Jamaica, the trend may have been started back in the Palm Suite.

I hope you have enjoyed reading about some of our funnier moments, or more aptly referred to as 'it will be alright on the night'. If you have never made a cocktail, these would be a good start as they are not too complicated. Give it a go; the more you make, the more the fun you have, although you might not remember them the next day. Cheers!

Champagne Cocktail

This is a rather expensive, flamboyant cocktail. I must stress, it is not the same if you cheat with some other cheap bubbles. This is one of the oldest cocktails dating back to the mid-1800s. The early cocktails did not have brandy in and is first mentioned as an option in the *Café Royal Cocktail* book in 1937. This sounds like a typically British cocktail and we certainly sold a lot to typically British people (and anyone else who wanted one!).

- 15ml brandy (good quality)
- 150ml Champagne
- 1 cube of white sugar
- Dash of Angostura bitters
- Garnish of small slice of orange and a cherry (optional)

Place the sugar cube in the champagne glass and carefully dash the Angostura bitters over the sugar lump.

Pour in the brandy, which should just cover the sugar, and top with the champagne.

Serve immediately for best impact.

Pina Colada

There are not many cocktails that have been sung about and turned into an international hit record. The record was called Escape (The Pina Colada Song) by Rupert Holmes and reached No.1 in December 1979. It surprisingly only reached No.23 in the UK, but it was a big hit at the Palm Suite Restaurant, played most evenings in the 80s. It has also featured in many films, including *Shrek* and *Guardians of the Galaxy*. It's a very jolly song and would be a great one to play as your party starts, possibly with a few Bob Marley hits too.

This is a sweet cocktail, but by adding a mixture of light & dark rums, it makes it a good grown-up drink. The Palm Suite coconut mix, which we did for 34 years, never changed and I think was one of our successes to this great version of one of our most popular cocktails. The combination of light and dark rums will make it a more authentic Caribbean drink and does improve the flavour. The recipe below has deleted the grenadine which turns it pink - this version was made by one of my first barmen by mistake! I hope the customer from the Caribbean has now recovered.

- 25ml light rum
- 25ml dark rum
- 425g tin cream of coconut
- 200g packet creamed coconut
- 50ml pineapple juice
- Good dash of Angostura bitters

The first thing you must do is prepare the coconut cream mix in advance. This may seem a little tedious but will improve the drink. Warm the tin and packet in a bowl of hot water to get the contents to room temperature so that it pours. Pour the contents into a bowl and add one full tin of water 425g. Whisk the mixture together, pour into a jug, with a lid if possible, and refrigerate. If it's too thick to your liking, just add a little more water.

When you are ready to make the drink, put about 4-5 ice cubes into a blender, add the rums, pour about 50ml of coconut cream mix so it smothers the ice. Then give a good dash of the Angostura bitters and pour in about 50ml of pineapple juice. This depends on how strong you want it and the size of the glass. Blend until the ice has stopped making a noise and the mixture is smooth. Pour into a glass dressed with fruit, 2 straws and a cocktail parasol.

Sip and sing to the Pina Colada song, *"Life's a beach."*

Harvey Wallbanger

This cocktail came about in the 50s in a bar on Sunset Boulevard and the story has it that a famous surfer called Tom Harvey ordered a screwdriver cocktail (vodka and orange juice) with a shot of Galliano on the top. He had not had a good day as he had a big wipe out in a surfing competition. Feeling rather fed up, he started to drink too many and got rather drunk. The next thing the bartender noticed was Tom knocking his head on the wall. So he named Tom's Cocktail "The Harvey Wallbanger". Good story; not sure if it's true.

At the Palm Suite, we had a single gentleman who regularly came in and ordered a takeaway BBQ Stilton Hamburger and, while he was waiting, we would pour him a Harvey Wallbanger. This routine went on for many years until one day he booked a table for 2 under the name of Harvey Wallbanger. That Saturday evening, he introduced us to his lady friend and we swiftly got his usual cocktail for him and the lady. The evening must have gone well as the pair of them became regular diners, continuing to always book under the name of Harvey Wallbanger.

I don't know if the ingredients played any part in their romance, but he did propose to her and they got married. I don't think she became Mrs Wallbanger, but he continued to book under that name so much so that the staff all forgot what his real name was.

A very simple cocktail to make but don't spoil it by floating too much Galliano on the top.

- 50ml vodka
- 100ml good fresh orange juice
- 25ml Galliano (or less)

Into a glass of your choice, add ice and pour in the vodka. Pour in the orange juice, leaving enough room to float the Galliano. Place in the straws, dress with fruit. Finish by floating the Galliano on the top. This, of course, slowly goes through the drink.

A must at the end of a good day's surfing, but perhaps not so good on a bad day, as Tom Harvey found out.

Picture above shown in a Hoffman German beer glass, which we used at the Palm Suite

Tropical Mai Tai

It is said that the cocktail was invented at a Trader Vic's bar in America. I have been to the one at the London Hilton on Park Lane. They serve a good variety of Hawaiian-style cocktails and food while you are surrounded by tropical plants and a bamboo. A great one to have on your must-go-to bar list. There are many different versions of this very refreshing long drink that originally was very citrusy. Our version is not quite so, as we have added orange juice and grenadine, but do add a reasonable amount of fresh lime juice.

- 25ml dark rum
- 25ml light rum
- 25ml orange curaçao or Cointreau
- Juice of one large fresh lime (this can be done in advance and stored in the fridge)
- 150ml freshly squeezed orange juice or a good quality carton juice
- 15ml orgeat (almond flavoured syrup) or use Amaretto for a stronger drink
- Dash of grenadine

Half fill a cocktail shaker with ice and pour in the spirits, followed by the juices and a dash of grenadine.

Place lid on firmly and give a good shake, then pour into a long glass of your choice.

Garnish with fresh lime and orange, with 2 straws.

Blue Lagoon

This fabulous-looking cocktail was a very good seller and as soon as we sold one, more orders would come in. I used to ask the waiting staff to walk round the restaurant with the drink before taking it to the table to pick up more sales of cocktails. The exotic blue colour in the liqueur, unfortunately, is only food colouring and not some exotic plant found on the Caribbean island of Curaçao. The drink itself is orange-flavoured liqueur.

I haven't a clue where I picked up this recipe, as the correct Blue Lagoon is vodka, blue Curaçao and lemonade, a weaker cocktail which is ideal if you have legally drinking teenagers at your party. This adult version has a bit more of a kick with the Drambuie and the tonic water is less sweet.

- 25ml blue Curaçao
- 25ml Tequila
- 20ml Drambuie
- Juice of ½ a small lemon
- 125ml good quality Indian tonic water

Half fill a cocktail shaker with ice and add the spirits and liqueur, plus the lemon juice.

Give shaker a good shake and pour over into a tall glass with the ice and fill with the tonic.

Garnish with a slice of orange and add straws (with optional maraschino cherry added in).

I can see somebody telling me now that the cocktail is not called a Blue Lagoon but that's what I called it in 1981 and nobody complained then, so it's the Palm Suite version of a Blue Lagoon. After a couple, you probably won't care what it's called!

Black Russian

This is a quick cocktail to make and gets its name from the use of Russian vodka, so be genuine and buy Russian. In hindsight, I don't think we ever did and we never had anyone complain that they did not get Russian vodka in their drink. It would have been a much better story if it was invented by the first black Russian bartender in his bar in Moscow, but it wasn't. I like the addition of a splash of coke on the top, and that was optional in the restaurant just in case we got a purest ordering one.

- 50ml good Russian vodka
- 25ml Kahlua
- 50ml Coke, Diet Coke or Coke Zero (your favourite brand)

Half fill a highball glass and pour over the vodka, then the Kahlua. Stir together.

Add a short straw and top with Coke if you desire a longer smoother drink.

White Russian

There are not many cocktails that have two versions and the White Russian is just as popular.

In a cocktail shaker with 4-5 ice cubes, add vodka, Kahlua and 40ml of whipping or double cream (whipping is better and the type of cream the bar always used).

Give the shaker a good shake and strain into a small martini glass. A superb after-dinner cocktail.

Make both drinks: Black before dinner and White afterwards, and then you should be ready for a bit of the famous Russian squat dancing. Better than Dad dancing!

Banana Banshee

This cocktail is definitely dessert in a glass and you can't go wrong mixing bananas and chocolate together. I am not sure where this drink originated, but it was certainly very popular in New Orleans and some bars made a screaming version by adding a large vodka. We never did the screaming drink, although I often felt like screaming at the bartender for taking so long to make this simple cocktail.

- 25ml white creme de cacao
- 25ml creme de banana
- 40ml whipping or double cream
- 1 x flaky type of chocolate for the topping

Place 4 cubes of ice in a cocktail shaker, pour over the spirits and cream.

Give a good vigorous shake and strain the drink into a small martini glass.

Then crush a small piece of the chocolate in a bowl until it becomes powder like, then sprinkle it over the top of the cocktail. This can be done in advance and stored in an icing sugar shaker.

Margarita Cocktail

The history of the Margarita is a little vague as so many bars and bartenders seem to claim fame to this somewhat unusual cocktail. In 1937 the Cafe Royal cocktail book has a recipe for a Picador with the same ingredients. The renaming of the cocktail seems to have happened in the hot southern states of America by Mexican barman. The popular assumption is that a Barman was making the drink for a 'Margaret' or a 'Margarita', which is Spanish for Daisy. I don't know who came up with the idea of putting salt round the rim of the glass but it does work. It may be because of the hot weather.

- 50ml tequila
- 25ml Cointreau or triple sec
- 35ml lemon or lime juice
- Salt for rimming the glass

Put a thin edge of salt on the rim of the glass. Wipe the top of the glass with lemon (lemon works much better than lime). Pour a small amount of salt onto a plate or saucer, hold the glass upside down and dip it in and turn the glass.

Then half fill your cocktail shaker with ice and pour in the tequila, Cointreau and juice. Give the cocktail shaker a good shake and strain into the centre of the glass so as to not to disturb the salt.

Do not pour in too much liquid as you must not get salt in the drink. Gently sip the cocktail through the salt.

In 1981 and the following few years, Palm Suite bartenders would always use Cointreau and lemon to make the drink. Then we did variations with lime and lemon & lime mix; all were good. We even made a Blue Margarita, replacing the Cointreau with blue Curaçao which is orange-flavoured.

Caution:

If you been diagnosed with high blood pressure or you are on medication for the symptoms, it is probably better to have it without the salt. The restaurant would serve a lot without salt.

Bloody Mary

Harry's New York Bar in Paris is supposed to be the birthplace of the Bloody Mary in 1921, which really started off as a large vodka, tomato juice and a squeeze of lemon. The important extras to this drink were first used at the St Regis Hotel in New York, which is now a luxury hotel built in 1904. This version came from a bar in Brooklyn which added horseradish and a dash of sherry. I am not sure any of them have ever cured a hangover but this one certainly wakes you up.

- 50ml vodka
- 15ml sherry
- 200ml tomato juice
- 1 tbsp tomato purée (optional)
- ½ juice of a lemon
- 2-3 dashes of Worcestershire sauce
- 6 drops of Tabasco
- 1 tsp horseradish sauce
- Shake of celery salt
- Garnish of fresh celery stick

Place all ingredients into a cocktail shaker with ice, shake for 20 seconds and strain into a long glass. Shake the celery salt on the top and garnish with a fresh celery stick.

There are many bars in the world called Harry's Bar, but the Harry's Bar in Venice invented the Bellini cocktail which is champagne and peach nectar and they are definitely not all the same Harry!

Grasshopper

Now, this elegant cocktail has some interesting history as it was invented at Tujague's Bar & Restaurant in the French Quarter of New Orleans in 1918. The bar and restaurant opened in 1856 and is still there today with its famous ornately framed French mirror.

- 25ml creme de menthe
- 25ml creme de cacao
- 40ml whipping or double cream
- Flaky milk chocolate

Place 4 cubes of ice in a cocktail shaker, pour over spirits and cream and give a good shake, then strain into a small martini glass.

Crush the chocolate into a powder in a small bowl and sprinkle over the cocktail. Can be done in advance and stored in an icing sugar shaker for easy use.

This is a really good after-dinner cocktail blending chocolate with mint, so forget about those minty matchsticks.

Brandy Alexander

The Palm Suite became quite famous for this cocktail as the film lads would often tell us ours was the best, and a lot of them did filming all over the world. We always used a good Spanish brandy and whipping cream, so maybe that made the difference. It originated around prohibition times in New York at the Hotel Rector. It then went on to be called The Hotel Claridge which closed in 1972 and was then demolished. That is a shame but this great cocktail lives on and is certainly one of my favourites.

- 40ml Spanish brandy
- 25ml dark creme de cacao
- 40ml whipping or double cream
- Nutmeg spice powder or freshly grated

In a cocktail shaker, place 4 cubes of ice, pour in brandy, cacao and cream and give a good quick vigorous shake until your hands feel cold.

Strain into a small martini glass and sprinkle over some nutmeg. We also did a large version of this cocktail which was double the ingredients.

Napoleon's Nightcap

I know I say this a lot, but this has to be my favourite after-dinner cocktail and it really does tick all the boxes. It's delightful to sip the brandy mixture through the minty cream.

It is an English cocktail that I spotted in the International Guide to Drinks compiled by the United Kingdom Bartenders' Guild. Now, that sounds posh even before you open the first page and I have to say, it's a must-have cocktail book. It's not published every year and the last one seems to be 2014. This great cocktail was the winner of the after-dinner selection of the National Cocktail Competition 1987. I think the drink was named after the brandy used, but we used our house brandy. Apparently, this particular well-known brandy was Napoleon's favourite. I doubt if he would know what brandy was used after being shaken with the other complementing ingredients. Anyway, Napoleon was certainly caught napping at the battle of Waterloo.

- 25ml brandy or Cognac
- 25ml brown crème de cacao
- 15ml crème de banane
- 20ml crème de menthe
- 20ml double cream

Place ice in your cocktail shaker and pour in the brandy, brown crème de cacao and crème de banane and give a good shake. Then strain into a cocktail glass.

Discard the ice from the shaker and pour in crème de menthe and cream, then give a good shake as that will thicken the cream.

Gently pour the cream mixture onto the back of a spoon above the glass, so it floats on top of the drink. If the cream is the right consistency, it will float easily.

Try this cocktail at your next dinner party. It looks good with the minty green top, it's easy to make and I find it livens the party up. They will want seconds!

Palm Sweets and Desserts

I never used to get too involved with the dessert menu and left it to my mother to do. In the early days, we would buy the odd one or two in from catering companies, but the most popular were the homemade. It made good sense to make them all so my mother was kept very busy, and with some regular help from my daughters, Emily & Jade, this was never a problem. This was their first experience in cooking and what a rewarding way to start and getting some pocket money too. As they got older and waitressed at the Palm Suite, they would see the diners eating and enjoying the desserts they had made.

A lot of our desserts would be popular dishes that you would see on many restaurant menus, such as the Sticky Toffee Pudding. Mother would often have her twist on the recipe which made the difference, where her toffee sauce and the lightness of the pudding certainly brought in lots of compliments. In the summer, mother's fresh Raspberry Cheesecake was often a best-seller and really worth the effort of making yourself. It will put you off buying them, particularly if you are entertaining and it's good fun trying out different flavours.

Cooking should always be enjoyable and all of our desserts can be prepared a day or two in advance which takes the pressure off, as the odd disaster won't matter. All this adds to the fun and hopefully the way to cook great dishes. I still keep my mother busy today as she makes the desserts for our family get-togethers, and she certainly hasn't lost the knack. We are sure you will also, very easily, get the knack for making Edna's great puds.

Sticky Toffee Pudding

My mother's homemade Sticky Toffee Pudding was one of her best desserts, which was always a big favourite with our customers. Her unique sauce using Demerara sugar and cream created a lighter toffee sauce.

Ingredients (serves 12 portions)

350g chopped dates
2 tsp instant coffee
275g sugar
275g butter
4 beaten eggs
1 tsp vanilla essence
400g self-raising flour
1 tsp bicarbonate of soda

Toffee sauce

225g butter
350g Demerara sugar
300ml cream

Method

1. Line a good-sized roasting tin (roughly 30cm x 35cm) with good quality cling film or greaseproof paper.
2. Cover the chopped dates with boiling water and add 2 tsp instant coffee.
3. Next, add the sugar and the butter followed by 4 beaten eggs and 1 tsp vanilla extract.
4. Fold in the self-raising flour with 1 tsp bicarbonate of soda. This will be quite a thin mixture.
5. Bake at 170°c for 25 - 30 minutes.

Toffee sauce

1. In a medium size saucepan, gently heat the butter and the brown sugar until melted.
2. Add 300ml cream carefully.

To serve

Cut into portions while still warm and pour over the heated toffee sauce and serve with cream or ice cream.

Raspberry Cheesecake

My mother made many different types of cheesecakes but this was one of the customers' favourites. Raspberries are now available in supermarkets all year round, but unfortunately, not a lot cheaper in season or from my wholesaler. I wanted to find a better way of buying raspberries as we were selling so much, so I tried a local farmer. He was very helpful, and also sold small buckets of broken and squashed raspberries, mainly to women making jam. You certainly don't need perfect raspberries for cheesecakes. So why not ask your local farmer what they do with their broken and squashed raspberries or pick your own? My mother always used cottage cheese which is healthier and does work well.

Ingredients (makes one cake, 10-12 slices)

600g cottage cheese

600g double cream

150g caster sugar

3tbsp or 24g gelatine

200g raspberries, sieved

200g digestive biscuits

125g butter

Method

1. Measure gelatine into a pouring jug, then pour in 200ml of boiling water and stir until it has dissolved and allow to cool.
2. While it's cooling, crush the digestive biscuits in a bowl using the end of a rolling pin.
3. Add the butter and work thoroughly together with your fingers (food handling gloves are a good idea for this sticky job).
4. Place the buttered biscuit into a greased 24cm baking tin and push firmly into the base and smooth off around the tin.
5. In a blender or food processor, place the cottage cheese and sugar, then blend until the mixture is smooth. You may have to blend in batches and mix together in a bowl.

6. Sieve the raspberries by pushing them through using the back of a soup ladle or similar.
7. Add the raspberry juice, cream and gelatine to the blender and blend until combined for 30 seconds, as you don't want to thicken the cream too much.
8. Leave in the fridge for 2 hours or until set.
9. With a very thin sharp knife, run it around the edge of the cake so when you open the tin, it comes away easily. Also, ease it off the base onto a serving plate.
10. Dress the top with raspberries and edible flowers if you like.

Blueberry Pancakes with Crème Fraiche and Raspberries

This dish could be breakfast or a dessert and it certainly sounds American. The British don't eat pancakes that often and they are rarely seen on menus. This version is easy to make and they are not stodgy. It pays to use good quality eggs, so try and get the ones that have the rich dark yellow yolk. Unfortunately, they do seem to be the most expensive, but hopefully, you are just about to make the best pancakes you have ever eaten.

Ingredients (serves 12)

3 medium free range eggs
250ml milk
100ml double cream
175g plain flour (preferably organic)
1 tsp paprika
Salt and pepper to season
200g blueberries

Method

1. Crack the eggs into a bowl and give them a good whisk.
2. Pour in milk and cream, then whisk into the eggs.
3. Sieve in the flour and whisk very thoroughly until the mixture is smooth.
4. Add paprika, salt and pepper, then whisk in.
5. Crush the blueberries in a bowl with a fork.
6. Add the crushed blueberries, stirring into the mixture.
7. Ladle the mixture into a small pancake pan.
8. Fry for a couple of minutes and turn over.
9. Place on a warm plate and store in a warm oven until all the pancakes are made.
10. Serve with crème fraiche and fresh raspberries.

Rhubarb, Raspberry and Pear Crumble

This is a different way to prepare a crumble, which did work very well at the restaurant. We would cook our fruit and crumble mix separately and combine the ingredients when we wanted to serve the dish. This way, we never served a sticky soggy crumble. The addition of pistachio nuts in the crumble mix really adds a new dimension to the texture.

Ingredients (serves 4 portions)

400g rhubarb chopped into 3mm chunks

4 medium firm pears (conference) peeled, cored and chopped

175g raspberries

50g sugar (for fruit)

150g demerara sugar for crumble mix

150g butter

250g plain flour (for crumble)

2tbsp flour (for fruit mix)

100g pistachio nuts chopped (optional)

Method

1. Place rhubarb and pears in a saucepan and coat with 2tbsp flour and add 2 tbsp water and the sugar. Simmer until the fruit is soft (about 8-10 minutes without a lid).
2. While the fruit cooks and cools, make your crumble. In a mixing bowl, rub the butter, flour and sugar with your fingers until it looks like breadcrumbs.
3. Thinly spread over a baking tray and place in the oven, cooking until they are light golden brown (roughly 10 minutes at 150°c.)
4. Remove crumble from the oven. When cool, mix with pistachio nuts.
5. When you are ready to serve, layer fruit in the bottom of the pie dish and mix in raspberries.
6. Top the fruit with the crumble mix and heat in a hot oven for about 10 minutes at 160°c, testing the centre by placing a skewer in the centre to see if it's hot.
7. When hot, serve in bowls with ice cream or custard.

Marshmallow Pie

This recipe came from my friend's restaurant, Joanna's. It's very quick and easy to make and looks very impressive with the pink and white layers. Make it in the morning so it sets nicely in the fridge.

Ingredients (serves 6 portions)

Half a packet of digestive biscuits - 250g crushed
110g salted butter
Approx. 40 white marshmallows
Approx. 40 pink marshmallows
200ml double cream
½ lemon

Method

1. Mix the crushed biscuits with the butter and pack into the base of a greased tin.
2. Mix the white marshmallows with 200ml double cream and slowly melt in the microwave together.
3. Squeeze ¼ lemon juice into the mix and then slowly pour onto the biscuit base and place in the fridge to set.
4. Once set, repeat with the pink marshmallows and place in the fridge to set.
5. To finish, dress with fresh fruits of your choice.

The Queen of Rice Puddings

This is one of my grandma's recipes, which is easily cooked in one hour with little effort. This recipe has half cream and half milk which gives the pudding a lovely creamy texture. The lemon zest and juice balances the pudding and makes it feel less stodgy. I hope you will stop buying the tinned versions and I'm sure you will think it's worth the effort. Add raisins or cranberries for a fruitier taste, with a little honey on the top.

Ingredients (serves 6 portions)

85g pudding rice

450ml double cream

450ml milk

30g butter

1 large egg

½ small lemon and zest

85g caster sugar

100g raisins or cranberries (optional)

A spoonful of honey (optional)

Method

1. Wash the rice in a sieve under cold water and put in a saucepan.
2. Add the butter, cream and milk, then stir together adding 30g caster sugar.
3. Heat until almost boiling and simmer for 40 minutes.
4. Let the rice cool; this can be sped up by putting the pan in cold water but be careful not to get any in the pudding.
5. Separate the egg yolk and beat. Then stir it into the rice with finely grated lemon zest. Add the raisins or cranberries if you are using them.
6. Turn the mixture into a large, buttered pie dish or 6 small ones. Whisk the egg whites with lemon juice and 55g caster sugar then pour over the puddings.
7. Place back in the oven at 170°c until the top browns and it is hot in the centre.
8. Test by placing a thin skewer into the centre and leave it for 10 seconds, then feel the end for hotness.
9. Cut out square sections and serve.

Brioche Bread and Butter Pudding

This is one of those great winter warming comfort desserts which we often did on the blackboard or on our winter menu. Making it with brioche is more expensive but worth it as it is lighter than bread. Finish the pudding by spreading with a good quality marmalade, or better still, a homemade one. I always raid my mother's cupboard for her homemade Seville marmalade which she makes each year when the Spanish oranges are in season.

Ingredients (serves 6 portions, using a pie dish 15cm x 22cm x 6cm high)

1 large brioche loaf
250ml milk
250ml double cream Salt
20ml vanilla extract
3 medium eggs
30g golden caster sugar
125g dried mixed fruit
150g salted butter (softened)
100g marmalade

Method

1. Pour the milk and cream into a large pan and bring to the boil.
2. Add vanilla extract and a teaspoonful of salt and whisk.
3. Let it infuse while cooling for 5 minutes.
4. Whisk the eggs and sugar together, then pour and whisk into the milk mixture.
5. While making the milk mixture, prepare the brioche by slicing thinly (1 - 1 ½cm) then cut each slice into 2 triangles and butter thinly.
6. Butter the dish and spread the fruit mixture on the bottom, followed by one layer of brioche triangles overlapping.
7. Repeat with the fruit mixture, then the brioche until the pie dish is full, finishing with brioche on the top layer.
8. Pour the cream mixture on the brioche and press down with a spatula. At this stage, you can cover and leave in the fridge before cooking. I have left it over- night and cooked it the next day when friends come round for dinner.

9. To cook, place the pudding dish in a larger roasting tin and half fill with water. Bake in the oven at 160°c for about 45 minutes until the top has started to brown but still feels wobbly.

10. Let it cool for 5 minutes or longer, then spread the marmalade over the top. Then place back into a hot oven at 180°c for about 10 minutes and it should rise. Serve with thick cream or custard.

Rachael's Chocolate Cake

One of my daughter's friends, Rachael, was raising money to go to Zambia to help build a school in a small village. She was desperate to raise funds and came up with this great idea for the restaurant to supply us with her family's homemade chocolate cake. After Rachael had raised the money, she gave us her family's secret recipe. This was a popular dessert which we religiously followed for years. The yoghurt was an important part of this recipe as it gave it a soft crumb texture. Dare I ever breathe the word microwave, the thick icing always looked too much but we gave each slice we cut a 30 second blast, just to make it start to melt and drizzle down the chocolate sponge.

Ingredients (serves 12 portions)

Chocolate Cake

225g self-raising flour
50g cocoa powder
1 tsp bicarbonate of soda
½ tsp salt
175g butter
275g caster sugar
3 beaten eggs
175g natural yoghurt

Icing

50g butter
50g cocoa
350g icing sugar
A dash of milk (if necessary)

Method

1. Sift the self-raising flour into a bowl then add the bicarbonate of soda and half a teaspoon of salt.
2. Next add the cocoa powder, and then blend with an electric whisk for 3-4 minutes.
3. Once blended, add 175g butter and 275g of sugar, then blend again for another 3-4 minutes.
4. In a separate bowl, beat 3 eggs and then 175g of natural yoghurt. Once blended, add to the flour mixture by stirring it in.
5. Line around 20cm tin with good quality cling film or greaseproof paper and pour in your mixture, then bake in the oven for one hour at 170°c.
6. While the cake is baking, make the icing. Soften butter on the hob and mix in with the cocoa and 350g icing sugar.

7. Add a dash of milk if it's too thick, to a creamy, spreading consistency.
8. Once the cake has cooled completely, place the icing on the top and sides using a spatula.
9. Refrigerate to harden chocolate.

To serve

1. Cut the cake into 12 portions (or less depending on choice of size).
2. Microwave for 30 seconds to warm and serve on a plate with cream or ice cream.

Rock n' Roll at the Palms

Over the years, the Palm Suite gained a great reputation for playing a good and interesting variety of music. This was heavily influenced by my love of rock and roll, particularly the 50s and 60s, and combining it with eating hamburgers, it seemed like the best music for the restaurant.

This was enjoyed by all ages, and much to my surprise, even the youngsters rated it! Tony James, a D.J. from Radio Luxembourg and a regular diner, said on one of his shows how good our hamburgers and music were, and "to get on down and give us a visit." He also recorded it for us, so we played it in the restaurant.

If you are making hamburgers at home, it has to be rock and roll music and one of my favourites is Eddie Cochran. Try his greatest hits album which will have *Three Steps to Heaven* on it, which was the last single record he released before the fatal car accident. After his tragic death in 1960 at the age of 21, *Three Steps to Heaven* went to number one.

I had a friend called Malcolm Cockren who worked at the film studios and wanted to make a film about Eddie Cochran. Ironically, he died before he made it. He had asked me to invest in the movie as well, and I'm sure having read the script it would have been a box office success. I hope one day it will be made as it would be a tribute to both of them.

Other good 50's rock and rollers are Gene Vincent, Buddy Holly, Elvis Presley, Ritchie Valens, The Champs, Chubby Checker, etc. On our side of the pond, you won't go wrong with The Beatles, The Who, The Rolling Stones, Yard Birds, The Kinks and Deep Purple. I hear dinner parties are having a bit of a revival, so I would recommend that Gourmet burger meal, sipping some of our Palm Suite cocktails with a bit of 50's - 60's rock and roll. I bet your guests would be talking about it for years! How about trying this for your three courses:

Crab Cakes with spicy mayonnaise

Cheese and Bacon Hamburger
With sauté potatoes, homemade coleslaw and a watercress salad

---

Marshmallow Pie
With peach purée and clotted cream

Some of my rock and roll favourites

My treasured Beatles collection

My mini recording studio at home

Although the restaurant was mainly frequented by film crew and stars, we did get quite a lot of people involved with the music business. This was often when they were involved in a film production or even doing some acting, or if they were using Pinewood stages for rehearsals.

We were thrilled when a local recording studio booked a table of 10 to celebrate Go West's new single. This good-looking 80's duo came as well and signed a copy of the latest album which I framed for the restaurant. I hope this helped them up the charts and they are still big performers today.

Elvis Costello, who was quite charming, came in for lunch but I have to say I knew little about him apart from that he made great hit records. Then I watched a documentary about his life which left me with loads of questions I would have loved to ask him. Always the way!

Myself and Sandy at the recording studios laying down our first release called "Swinging in the Palms." All proceeds went to Live Aid and we were all wearing our Palm Aid t-shirts!

I was discussing music one lunch with John and a few regular customers and John suggested I should also play some relaxing instrumental music at lunch, such as Country Airs by Rick Wakeman. I then ordered a copy of the CD for the restaurant. By coincidence, two weeks later, Rick Wakeman, with his long flowing blond hair, walked into Palm Suite. This was great as John had also called by for some lunch. Of course, we found him a nice table and after his meal he came to the bar and chatted to John and I. John mentioned how much he enjoyed the Country Airs album which we were playing at the time. His reply was, "Did I record that?" If you'd made as much good, varied music as Rick Wakeman, it would be hardly surprising you couldn't remember it! I think he was joking but he was a very nice guy.

Sheila Ferguson had lunch with us and I was asked to sit down and join them. If I was ever invited on Desert Island Discs, *When Will I See You Again* would probably be my number one. Sheila did sign her latest album cover for me.

The great American Hamburger gets everywhere!

Somebody who must be very high up the rock n' roll hall of fame must be Jimmy Page from Led Zeppelin. He certainly had an immediate presence as he entered the restaurant with a young lady. He clearly didn't want to talk me or any of my staff. I didn't think he was in a good mood or maybe he had even had an argumentwith his young lady. They had their meals, downed a couple of drinks and left, but still a great boast to say you had Jimmy Page in your restaurant. I wish he had done something outrageous as some rock n' rollers do.

I did once get told by a Pinewood driver that the hamburger takeaway was for a Stevie Wonder who was rehearsing at Pinewood for some pop festival.

That's the Palm Suite's and Palm Court's (our other restaurant at Maidenhead) small but interesting Rock n' Roll Hall of Fame. I would also like to thank Ken, a very regular customer for many years, who gifted me his mint condition complete set of all the Beetles' albums, which gave me and many of our customers many hours of listening pleasure.

Go West came in for lunch celebrating the release of their first album and signed their album cover for the restaurant. I am sure we helped their album get high in the charts with our non-stop playing!

Good old-fashioned L.P. albums. Now gaining a lot of interest again and being produced.

The customers loved to hear Elvis so we booked a couple of tribute acts!

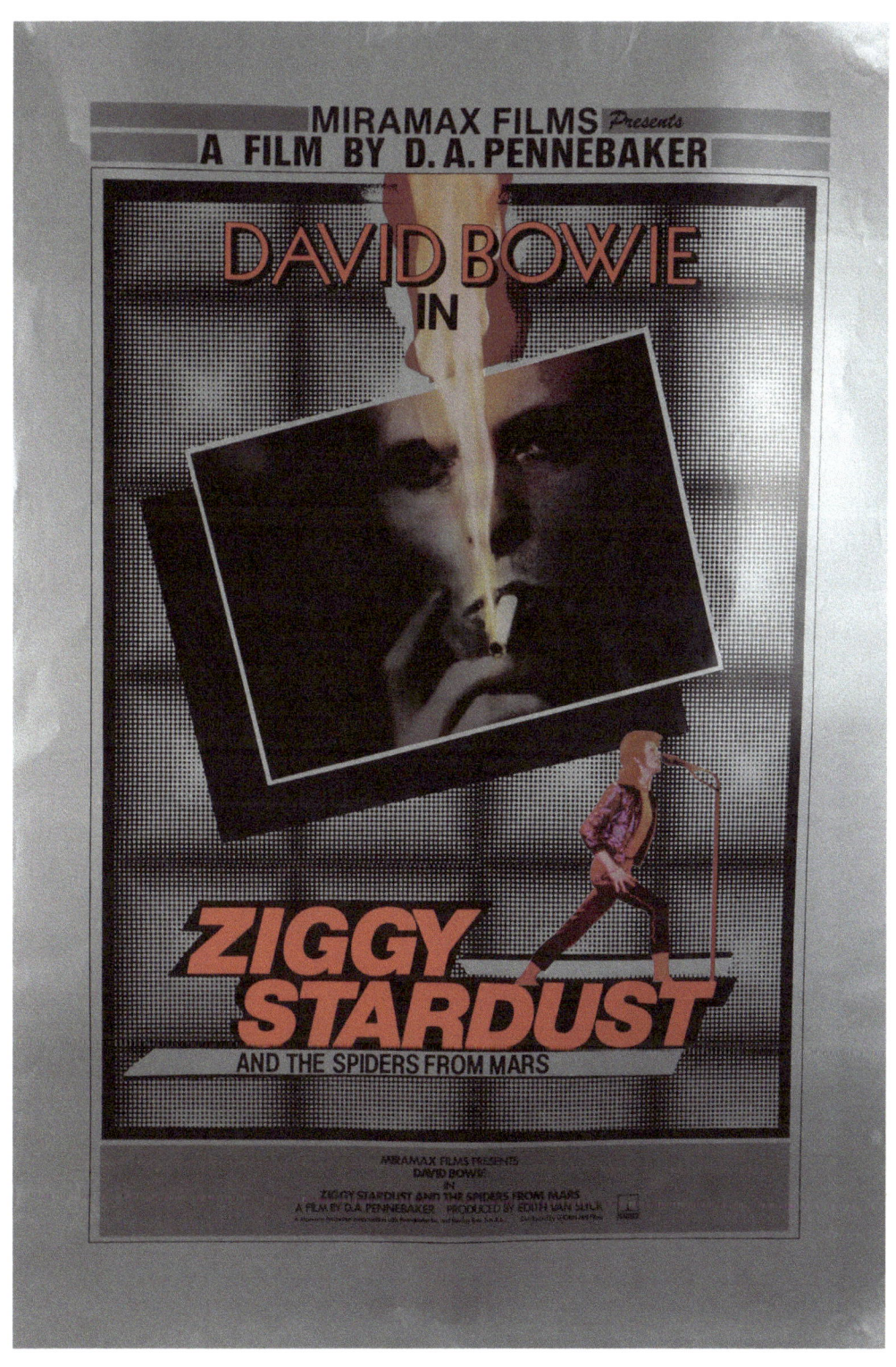

This movie took years to make and was finally released in 1983, corresponding with the release of its soundtrack album called Ziggy Stardust: The Motion Picture

The Palm Court, Restaurant Number 2

This is not an easy profession to go into but I would always encourage anyone who was serious about it and has done their research with the right vision to go for it! I was always very proud that over the years, several of my staff left the Palm Suite to open their own restaurants with various amounts of success. I had a vision of owning a chain of successful restaurants, so my mother and I doubled our challenge and problems just 2 years after opening Palm Suite.

We bought our second restaurant in Maidenhead and had to pay a premium for it back then, something you wouldn't necessarily have to do today. We called it 'Palm Court Restaurant' and gave it a music theme with instruments hanging from the ceiling. I went to musical instrument shops and would buy their unwanted broken ones, which they were pleased to get rid of cheaply. I converted the drums into hanging baskets and even put up a double bass. Palm Court had a good selection of pictures on the walls including rare pictures of the original Palm Court Orchestra with large potted palms.

We had our usual realistic-looking fake palm tree in the middle of the restaurant with tables underneath the branches. In next to no time, the restaurant became very popular and was often full on midweek evenings. I would often start the evening at Palm Suite, then go to Palm Court.

Palm Court was the bigger restaurant, seating 60, and the layout of it lent itself to fun party theme nights which turned out to be more popular than at Palm Suite. As Palm Court was themed as the musical restaurant, I thought it was time to have some live music. We had a piano shop next door to us who sold me one of their rare cheap trade-ins for £300.00. I then hired a jazz pianist for Saturday nights and this went down a storm and we started to almost get too busy. The local paper wrote up about all that jazz at the Palm Court, which boosted trade even more, particularly on quiet nights.

One day, I was chatting to the chefs about new dishes, when suddenly, one of them interrupted and asked had I ever had a singing guitarist in the restaurant. "No, do you know one?" He replied, "Yes, me! I do down my local pub when I am free." So he brought his guitar in and did a demo for Edna and me. He was great, so we booked him for the following week and billed him as our singing chef. I advertised the event in the local newspaper and the bookings soon rolled in until we were full.

The big night came, so our singing chef started off in the kitchen dressed in his full white uniform and hat. We had our other chefs doing most of the cooking and he just stood in our open kitchen passing the plates out to the waitresses, looking very important. Then, at the right moment, out he came, guitar in hand, singing to our diners. This went down

The night I joined our singing chef for one of his famous performances!

All that jazz at the Palm Court

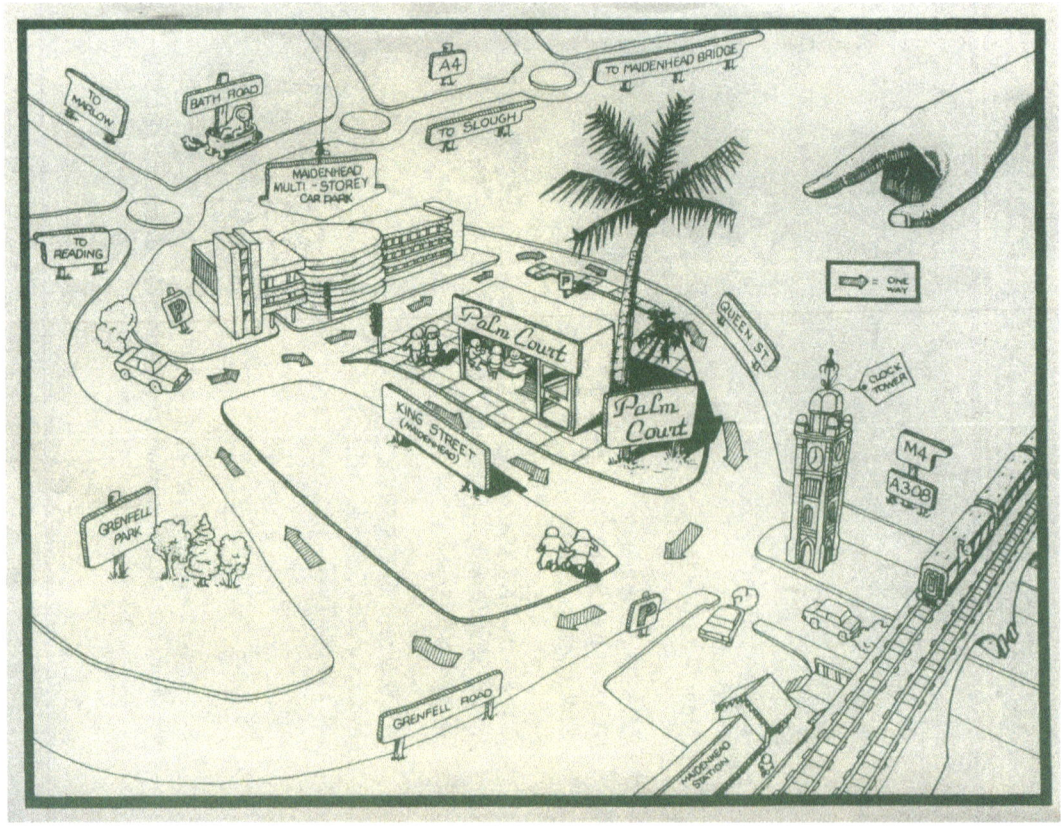

really well and they were soon singing along and giving great applause. He was to do three 30-minute slots in and out of the kitchen. By the third at the end of the evening, most of the diners were up dancing. As he got towards the end and thanking everyone and me, he decided to call me up to do a song with him! Now, I can't sing and am tone deaf, but there was no going back. He had chosen a rock 'n' roll number, so I knew the words. With a few Elvis type moves, I got through it. I don't think I deserved the applause but it was great fun that evening.

I remember one Thursday evening we were busy in both restaurants. Palm Court had a big party down the middle of the restaurant next to the palm tree. Everything was running well and the last meals had just been served. The manager was doing an excellent job, so off home I went at 10.30pm. I hadn't been in long when the phone rang, and a rather flustered manager said, "David, you will have to come back. The palm tree is on fire!"

"What?! I am on my way." I lived locally so I was back in minutes and sure enough, there was Ken, my friend and barman, trying to put out the flames with wet tea towels. We soon had it out, but we didn't have much palm tree left.

I asked Ken how it started and he told me they were smoking; the chap lit the dry coconut bark with his lighter and it caught fire very quickly. "He's at the bar if you want to talk to him." He was with the group that was sitting under the palm tree having a drink. I went straight up to him and before I could say anything, he told me our palm tree was a fire hazard. "What?!" I said, "Anything is a fire hazard if you set fire to it. That chair is a fire hazard with your lighter underneath it." They soon left, although I did feel like chucking them out, but at least they paid.

My friend John had given me his unwanted palm tree which went in the next day, so we kept quiet about the event and obviously never informed our customers about our 'fire hazard' tree. It never happened again and I sprayed the bark with fire repellent liquid too, just in case.

Palm Court was a bit unlucky with fires, as another night I got a call from the local Fire Brigade at 2.00am, telling me the restaurant was on fire. Again, I arrived in minutes to find the hose pipes were putting out the flames from our recycling cardboard storage unit underneath the cooking extraction. The flames had travelled down the extraction into the kitchen, filling the restaurant full of smoke. There was a lot of smoke damage. The police were there as well and I asked how it had happened. Apparently, they had arrested someone who was nearby smelling of white spirit and with a large box of matches. "Good evidence," I said, "well done," trying not to sound sarcastic. "Well, we won't be pressing charges as he's mentally not well. He informed us he had a message from God to burn down these sinful places selling alcoholic drink. The bookmakers up the road had also been set on fire."

This closed us for five weeks. The local papers reported on it, but I made sure I informed them how it happened so it wouldn't affect trade when we reopened. Thankfully, it didn't and we were having reopening parties, although you could still smell the smoke (just as well you could still smoke in restaurants back then anyway).

We had Palm Court for 10 years, and although it was very successful, it never had the glam of being next door to a film studio with a constant stream of celebrities. Then, out of the blue, someone came along and offered me money to buy the restaurant. This would give me some capital to extend and improve Palm Suite, so I did the deal and left Maidenhead. The restaurant remained as Palm Court for a further 15 years and a lot of my staff stayed on, but I don't think he had quite the same success as we had in the 80s.

Back to one Palm

The sale of Palm Court happened in November, 1992, so the new owner had a good start with the Christmas trade. We had a very good Christmas at Palm Suite with a lot of large parties from Pinewood Studios. It was certainly a lot easier running one restaurant which helped my family life, as we had two daughters, Emily (aged 3) and Jade (aged 2), with another baby on the way.

After the early recession in the 90s, the Palm Suite and Pinewood Studios started to pick up nicely. The film stars and film crews were soon back lunching at the restaurant and Pinewood were taking in television productions as well. The restaurant became very popular with The Minder series film crew, led by a chap called Ken, who seemed to have his own chauffeur. They would often go out for a morning location recce that would end with lunch at the Palm Suite. As usual, we would get a phone call to tell us anything up to 20 wanted a table in half an hour. We always said yes and then had the challenge of sitting them on one long table while in service.

The main star and character in The Minder was a chap called George Cole. One of the crew had spotted an old black & white film picture on the wall of a wedding scene from The Constant Husband. This had a very young George Cole in it and also star Rex Harrison who had signed the picture. They asked me if they could borrow it to make George a Christmas card from the crew. Of course I said yes and unscrewed it from the wall. He really appreciated the card and they had printed an extra picture, which George signed to the Palm Suite. I then put up both pictures; another good story to tell the diners.

The 90s were good years for the restaurant and my mother and I built up a good strong staff team as she started to go into semi-retirement. Mother was always at hand to help us with the food ideas and would prep and make a lot of food for the restaurant including the famous Steak & Kidney pies and her amazing desserts.

I was still working lunch and evening which was not very conducive to a stable marriage, and sure enough, I wound up adding to the number of restaurateurs in the divorce courts. I did get the pleasure of sharing the children, unlike a lot of fathers who rarely see their family. My life was good with the three children and if I was at the restaurant, my mother was there to help.

To run a restaurant, I think you have to be fit mentally and physically, and I always considered myself lucky as I had no problems. Well, that was until 2003, when I was told I had cancer. Everybody at the restaurant rallied around and off I went for a very successful operation, so it wasn't long before I was back working.

Yes, I was one of the very lucky ones.

I viewed running the restaurant in a different way and appreciated its success even more. This I shared with my children who enjoyed working at the restaurant. Their career ideas stretched further than mine and the film industry looked more appealing than restaurants. The Palm Suite connection with Pinewood Studios certainly helped them all. They are actively working in film & television and it's lovely to hear when they meet restaurant customers from Pinewood Studios who often send their regards to me.

The Palm Suite had many good years in the 2000s as well, but like all things in life, we get change that we do not want. After the banks crashed in 2008, working life started to change and the idea of popping out for lunch and an alcoholic drink was becoming frowned upon. At first, this didn't affect the film industry, which seemed recession proof and unlikely to change. The American film production companies were getting more interested in making movies in the UK and at Pinewood. That was the good news. The bad news for me was that they were not keen on them having lunch out. At first, the Palm Suite regulars didn't take too much notice, so contracts were changed with straight 10-hour shifts and with 'no alcohol' clauses. It was rumoured they even threatened breathalysers on employees who appeared to have been drinking, and testing positive would have meant instant dismissal.

Slowly but surely, our lunchtime trade started to drop away apart from the odd end-of-shoot lunch and John Grover, now a retired film editor, who would meet his fellow film chums for their monthly lunch get-together. There was also a locations guy, Chris, who enjoyed the occasional glass of red wine at the Palm Suite and would often remind me that I had banned him from the restaurant in the 80s, accusing him of being drunk and too loud. I don't remember that as he was one of our favourite interesting lunch customers. We also had a film sound company that occasionally had time for lunch at the Palm Suite. I nearly forgot to mention a more senior, very smart gentleman who owned a local company who would lunch most days on soup of the day and a glass of wine. There unfortunately turned out to be many a lunch where it was just the two of us. I ticked along like this for a few years and although we were still busy in an evening, the lunchtime excitement had gone. I started to doubt whether I was any good at being a restaurateur anymore and felt like a washed-up has-been.

I had also been through a case of somebody suing me for falling over a large flower pot outside the restaurant while on his phone. I lost the case costing me a lot of money. In fact, it was about £25,000 that his no win, no fee solicitors cost me, which was devastating for me at the time.

I worked the last Saturday night which was a quiet one and went in on Monday morning and shut the restaurant. I have often looked back with some regret and sadness, as I am sure having farewell parties would have been good. I was surprised at the time to receive so many kind messages from customers telling me of their sadness to see the restaurant close and how much they had enjoyed dining at the Palm Suite.

Life's journey has many twists and turns, but the time was right for me to hand the restaurant to someone new. My wine supplier told me that one of their Italian customers was interested in getting another restaurant. The same week I closed, they viewed the restaurant and the deal was done; La Palma Restaurant was born. I have to say I was extremely pleased with their choice of name. I still run Palm Suite Accommodation for the film technicians which keeps me busy, as Pinewood has expanded and filled up with movie-makers.

My next project is with Carole, the love of my life and best friend, the perfect partner. We were away on holiday on a romantic Greek island and bought a big old run-down house. The plan is to do it up, and for us and our 6 children to have many dream holidays (and also a few holiday lets at mate's rates!). We have a long way to go, as rain pours in on the occasional storm and a pipe has burst under the ground. Upstairs is well ventilated, with cracks the size of your hands.

Yes, a big project and maybe our next book...

Still swinging between the palms....

PRESS RELEASE

2nd June 1981

PALM SUITE RESTAURANT OPENING
SOON IN IVER HEATH

ANYBODY WITH AN EYE FOR EXCITING INNOVATIONS WILL BE AT THE OPENING NIGHT OF THE PALM SUITE RESTAURANT, ST. DAVIDS CLOSE, IVER HEATH ON 16TH JUNE 1981.

ITS NOT - EXPENSIVE, FORMAL, 'WEAR A TIE', STAID, BORING OR EVEN JUST ANOTHER HAMBURGER JOINT.

IT IS - (AND THIS IS THE GOOD NEWS) LIVELY, INFORMAL, TRENDY, WITH COCKTAILS - PINA COLADAS; STEAKS, BURGERS, CLAMS, CHILLI, ALL PRICED SO THAT YOU DON'T FEEL LIKE YOU'RE BUYING THE PLACE, ONLY THE MEAL!

PALM SUITE WILL BE OPEN FOR PLEASURE, LUNCHTIMES MONDAY TO FRIDAY AND EVENINGS TUESDAY TO STAURDAY. TELEPHONE IVER 652100.

PALM SUITE - THE PLACE TO BE SEEN.

FOR FURTHER DETAILS PLEASE CONTACT JULIET OR EDNA WILLIAMS ON EITHER IVER 652100 OR MAIDENHEAD 32332.

Illustration to advertise our business lunches

Waitress on Nouveau Beaujolais eveni[ng]

Palm Suite
Christmas menu

2 Course Festive menu - £17.00
3 Course Festive menu - £22.50

Starters - £5.50

V Roast Cherry tomato soup with a swirl of basil oil
Prawn Cocktail with homemade Marie-rose sauce
Mussels in cider cream and thyme served with crusty bread
Tempura battered goat's cheese and beetroot jam
Crispy pork on a sweetcorn fritter, coriander salad, sweet chilli sauce

Main Courses - £11.50

Butter poached bronzed Turkey with chestnut & turkey leg stuffing, bacon chipolatas & all the trimmings with rich homemade gravy

Melting roasted lamb slowly cooked with paprika and oranges. Served with herb mash, peas and carrots

Fillet of sea bass on wilted spinach with orange and cointreau butter sauce served with new or sauté potatoes

V Wild Mushroom, Spinach and Walnut Wellington with blue cheese sauce, mixed vegetables and choice of potatoes

Chicken breast stuffed with leeks and boursin, roasted cherry tomato sauce and choice of potatoes

Desserts - £5.50

Homemade Christmas pudding, brandy and fresh cream
Dried cherry and chocolate bread pudding with custard
White chocolate and baileys cheesecake with cream or ice cream
A selection of blue cheeses & biscuits

All menus are interchangeable
½ price for children 12 years and under

Open for Lunch and Dinner Monday to Saturday. Available for private functions on Sundays. An optional service charge of 10% will be added to...

"Just when you thought it was safe to go back into the lost resort of Iver Heath"

PALM SUITE RESTAURANT BITES BACK
with its devastating new menu!!

starring

The Mouthwatering Swordfish Steak

co-starring

Oriental Wun-Tun

and

The Delectable Passion Cake

Special Star Appearance

The Seductive Sweetdreams Cocktail

Plus many other new and exciting attractions

Tel. IVER 652100
for your booking

COCKTAILS

A selection of our favourite drinks offering good strength and balance for your enjoyment. Cheers

£3.65 SELECTION

MAMANS CHARM Amaretto, Kahlua, ... and Coconut Cream
MAMANS COOLER Light rum, Blue ..., Ginger Ale, Lime, Gomme
HARVEY PUDPUCKER Tequila, Galliano, Orange Juice
BLOODY MARY Vodka, Tomato Juice, ...

£4.20 SELECTION

BARRACUDA Light Rum, Galliano, Pineapple Juice & Sparkling Wine
MELON SMUGGLER Vodka, Midori, Peach Liqueur, Lime & Pineapple Juice
EMERALD ICE Light Rum, Melon Liqueur, Galliano, Lime Juice
PLAYMATE Brandy, Apricot Liqueur, ..., Angostura, Orange Juice

CREAM COCKTAILS
(particularly good after a meal)

ALL AT £3.60

BRANDY ALEXANDER Brandy, Creme de Cacao, Cream, topped with Nutmeg
BANANA BANSHEE Creme de Banane, White Creme de Cacao sprinkled with Chocolate
GRASSHOPPER Creme de Menthe, White Creme de Cacao topped with Flaky Chocolate
PINK PANTHER Bourbon, Malibu, Vodka, Grenadine and Cream
WHITE RUSSIAN Kahlua, Vodka and Cream finished with a sprinkling of chocolate
NAPOLEON'S NIGHTCAP extra 0.75 Brandy, Creme de Cacao, Creme de Banane, finished with Creme de Menthe & Cream
MIDNIGHT COWBOY Gin, Kahlua, Cream served in a long glass topped with coca-cola
LIQUEUR COFFEES Irish, Jamaican, 2.50 French, Calypso, Russian, Scotch. All topped with fresh whipped cream

MOCKTAILS
(NON-ALCOHOLIC)

COCONUT CRUSH Coconut Cream, ..ple Juice and Cream
BANANA SHUFFLE Orange Juice, ..dine, Cream and fresh Banana
TONGA Fresh Pineapple, Pineapple Grenadine and Lemonade
BARBARELLA'S FRUITELLA Grapefruit, Pineapple, Lime Juice and Grenadine
VIRGIN MARY Tomato Juice, Lemon, Worcester Sauce, Tabasco, topped Celery Salt
FUSSYFRUIT Fresh Pineapple, Praise, Orange and Lemon Juice Grenadine

PURE FRUIT JUICES
SPARKLING MINERAL WATER 1 Litre Bottle
SOFT DRINKS AND DIET C...

SPIRITS

SPIRITS from	1.65	
with mix or juice	2.40	
COGNAC V.S.O.P.	2.50	
PORT L.B.V.	2.25	
JACK DANIELS OR WILD TURKEY	2.00	
SAMBUCA WITH COFFEE BEANS	2.30	
COINTREAU OR GRAND MARNIER	2.20	
SOUTHERN COMFORT	2.20	
LIQUEURS		
... a good range from	2.00	

BEER

For our latest full range international beers, please look at the blackboard above bar

---

PALM SUITE
CHRISTMAS SPECIALS

Starts Monday 2nd December
Lunch and Dinner three course
£14.70

Turkey and Cranberry Soup.
£3.25

Homemade Salmon Pate with French bread.
£3.25

Smoked Chicken Salad with Mango & Lime Dressing.
£3.25

Beef Steak with Port Wine Sauce. scotch sirloin thinly sliced, marinated & grilled.
£7.95

Grilled Breast of Chicken.
with a leek & cream cheese sauce.
£7.95

Fillet of Red Snapper with Red Pepper Relish. lightly seasoned with herbs & spices.
£7.95

All served with a choice of potatoes a.q. or rice or salad.
Vegetarian dishes on main menu.

Christmas Pudding with Rum & Orange Sauce.
£3.50

Ginger Meringues with Pear & Chocolate Sauce.
£3.50

Good House Wine
£7.50

THE DISHES ARE PRICED INDIVIDUALLY

Oh dear, I really do think we should go to the Palm Suite this year.

Palm Suite

Palm Suite Restaurant
Within Shooting Distance of the Film Business

WINES AND COCKTAILS

Palm Suite
RESTAURANT
St. David's Close, Iver Heath, Bucks.
Telephone: (01753) 652100

WHITE WINES

Concha Y Toro Sauvignon Chardonnay (Chile) — 8.50
From the Pirque Vineyard, fresh, crisp, with a gooseberry finish exceptionally good value

Niersteiner Gutes Domtal Schloss Kellerei — 8.25
Good fruity medium style wine

Hardy's Nottage Hill Chardonnay — 12.50
Australia's flag ship vineyard offers the full bodied dry wine with lots of fruit and oak overtones

4. Frascati Superiore — 8.75
Classic Italian wine, fresh, dry, zingy taste

5. Bourgogne Aligoté AC — 12.75
Excellent quality dry wine with mellow grapefruity flavour, long finish

6. House White — 7.35
Inexpensive easy drinking dry wine

By the glass 125ml — 1.65

RED WINES

8. Club Claret Bordeaux AC — 9.25
Light red, spicy notes with soft blackcurrant flavours

9. Beaujolais Superieur – Chateau du Grand Talancé — 9.95
A good quality soft round fruity wine

10. Concha Y Toro Cabernet Sauvignon — 8.75
A New World wine from Chile, a well balanced red with a spicy blackcurrant taste

11. Rioja, Siglo Saco Tinto — 11.25
Tile red ...

12. Vino Vo... Peter L... —
Velvety red ... character...

14. Antigua... Vino Casablanca...
From Chile's ... famous wines... very aromatic... length, excep...

15. House Red
Good value...

By the glass 1...

CHAMPAGNE

17. Maison Champagne
Round fresh, good quality, well balanced with yeasty flavour
By the glass

LOOK WHAT'S NEW AT PALM SUITE

B.B.Q. SMOKED CHICKEN & RIBS

Lightly smoked over Hickory Woodchips, then cooked mighty slow in our delicious B.B.Q. Sauce, that creates a unique mouthwatering flavour.
The restaurant famous for steaks, burgers and fish can now boast Heap Big Chicken & Ribs.

**Blaze a trail to Palm Suite Restaurant.
Rustle up a tribe or just bring Siou...**

Palm Suite Restaurant

MEANS BUSINESS

Entertaining or just a quick lunch, we can do it, with prices that won't upset your cash flow or the boss.

We clock in again at 6 o'clock. A tasty appetiser or the full works — Palm Suite has it for you.

Lunch — Mon.-Fri. 12.00-3.00
Dinner — Mon.-Sat. 6.00-11.30

Accounts always considered

52 St. David's Close, Bangors Road North
Telephone: 652100

LOOK WHAT'S NEW AT PALM SUITE

B.B.Q. SMOKED CHICKEN & RIBS

Lightly smoked over Hickory Woodchips, then cooked mighty slow in our delicious B.B.Q. Sauce, that creates a unique mouthwatering flavour. The restaurant famous for steaks, burgers and fish can now boast Heap Big Chicken & Ribs.

NEW STAR LINE-UP...

Kick Off this Week with our Exciting New Menu.
— You've got to be on a Win

- ☆ DEEP FRIED CAMEMBERT
- ☆ BARBECUED BEEFSTEAK
- ☆ CHICKEN CHASSEUR
- ☆ SALMON STEAKS
- ☆ BABY BACK RIBS
- ☆ BROCHETTE OF LAMB
- ☆ ½ A BARBECUED CHICKEN
- ☆ CASPER WINEBURGER
- ☆ TUNA FISH SALAD
- ☆ BLACKCURRANT & IC
- ☆ ST. CLEMENTS SUN

Palm Suite
St. Davids Close, Iver Heath, Bu
Tel: Iver 652100

Palm Court
57 King Street, Maidenhead, B
Tel: Maidenhead 781212

A song for Africa courtesy of Palm Aid

Aid, from left: Tracy Whittle, Laura Kelly, Linzi Hollidge and Amanda Weeks.

PALM PEOPLE presents **'SWINGING IN THE PALMS'**

Come and hear our new song for sale only at Palm Restaurants

Palm Aid 1985

Slip into a Palm Aid T-shirt
Enter the Great Palm Aid competition
BOOK YOUR TABLE NOW

Palm Suite
Iver Heath
0753 652100

Me making a speech at the 5 year annviersary, I bought my jacket from Bloomingdales in New York. We're not too sure what the parrots are doing!

The Palm Suite's window poster promoting Valentines night

Leek & Potato Soup 2.25
Palm Sweet
Sticky Toffee
Pudding
3.25

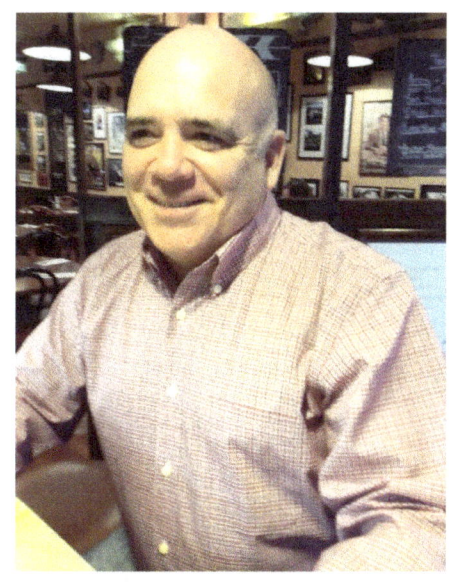

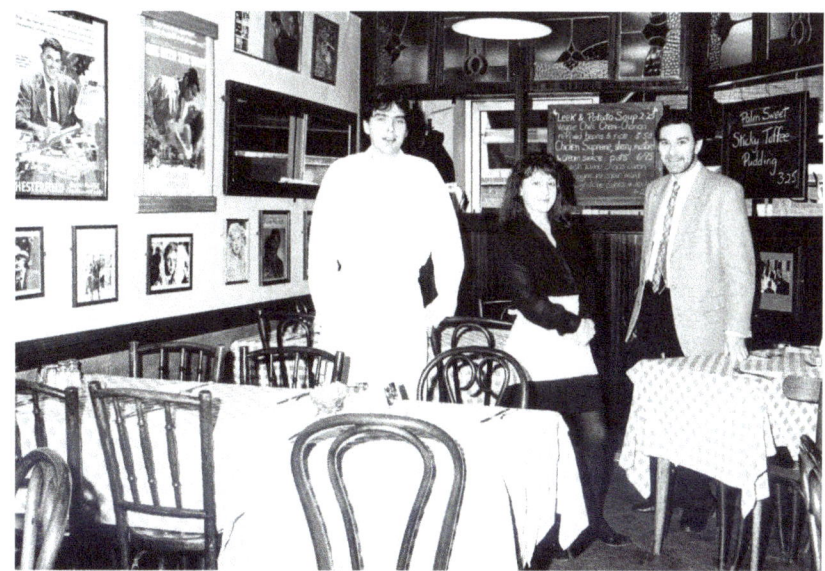

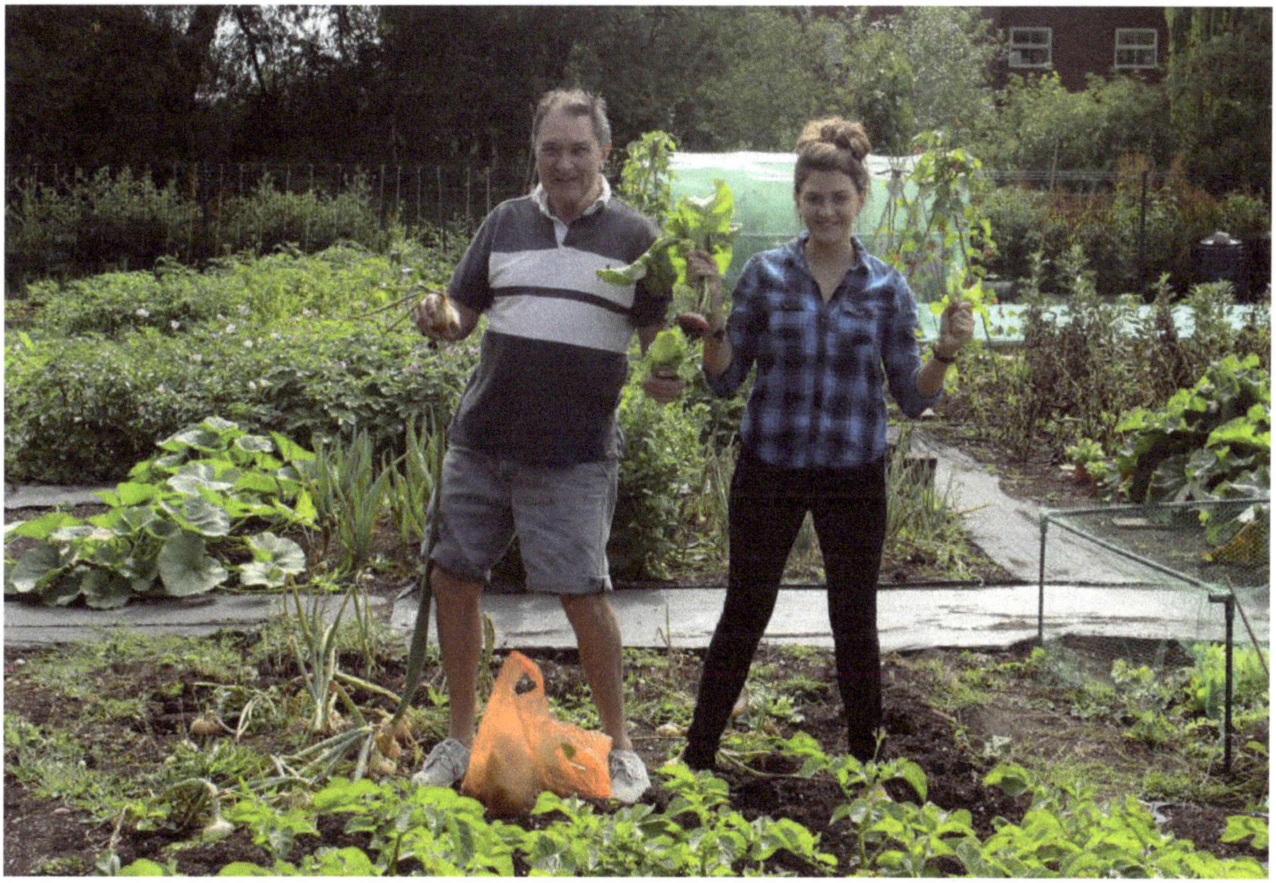

Acknowledgements and Special Thanks

This turned out to be the hardest page to write as there are so many of you to thank. So I thought I would do it in order of how the book started.

After I made that incredibly hard decision to close Palm Suite with no farewell parties, which in many ways I regret, I am sorry as I'm sure you would all have made it so good.

After we closed, Carole encouraged me to write a book about some of my experiences over the 34 years of owning Palm Suite. Thank you for your support, hours of reading and correcting my bad grammar, and most importantly, being the love of my life.

Next is Jade, (daughter and our last manageress) who spent so many hours, which turned into days and weeks, collating the book together. Draft after draft, your patience never ran out. I can't thank you enough.

Daniel, (son and great cocktail barman). Thank you for all your fabulous photographs in the book.

Emily, (daughter and Palm Suite manageress). Thank you for the hours you spent cooking the recipes and making sure they worked. Your involvement and support has been second to none.

Katie, who joined the Palm Sweetie waitresses and then did an English degree at university. You also became a marketing executive and spent many hours using all these amazing skills to help us finish editing the book and correcting my grammar.

Laurence, for helping me kick-start the book with the soup recipes and sharing his love of Rock n' Roll music.

Robert, my brother, who I have to thank for his amazing ability to consistently cook great food for 11 years.

Pete, thank you for accidentally applying for the waiter's position and letting me talk you into the job. You were the best all-rounder who lived round the corner from me and became the 'free taxi' for my children taking them back and forth from Palm Suite. Also, for teaching them how to eat kebabs at 1 am in the morning. Often known as Pete the Greek, who has just helped me to buy a big old rambling house on a Greek island, another book maybe…

Daniel Williams - our book photographer. Thank you so much for the many hours of work you put into making these photos great (and for putting up with me!)

Thank you to the following companies who played a major role in supplying Palm Suite:

Sean - Heanens Butchers, Roehampton, London

Steve and team - WBK Catering, supplying all the cocktail glasses

Father to sons – Brown's Seafood suppliers of our fresh fish

Carole's- Home-grown fruit and vegetables exclusive to the Palm Suite

I now need to give a very special thanks to all the staff from the most important wash-ups to the chefs, waiting, bar staff and managers. This may sound strange now but I loved working with you all and you all helped make Palm Suite the amazing restaurant it became.

Last but not least, the thousands upon thousands of customers who enjoyed our food, drink and rock n' roll, creating that perfect atmosphere that would make any restaurateur proud.

Index

A

Cream of Asparagus soup: 122

B

Cheese & Bacon Skins: 144

Beef:
Strip Cut Sirloin: 148–149
Peppered Fillet Steak: 178–179
Steak Kebabs in Oyster Sauce: 180-181
Edna's Homemade Individual Steak & Kidney Pudding: 196–199

Beef burgers:
The Bacon and Cheese burger: 97
Blue Stilton and BBQ sauce burger: 98
Rob's burger: 100

Beef meatballs:
Aromatic Beef Meatballs with fresh Tomato Sauce: 166–167

Beef ribs:
Barbecue ribs: 172–173

C

Coleslaw: 102

Cheese:
Broccoli and Stilton soup: 120
Goats cheese croutons: 130
Cheese & Bacon Skins: 144
Roquefort sauce: 170–171

Chicken:
Chicken Burgers topped with Beetroot Relish and Goats Cheese: 107–108
Chicken Satay: 135
Buffalo Chicken Wings with Blue Cheese Dip: 140–141
Thai Poached Chicken Salad with Tahini dressing: 153–154
Grilled Chicken Breast with Ginger Mint Butter: 182-185
Sweet & Sour Chicken: 200–201

Jamaican Jerk Chicken with Banana and Papaya Ketchup: 158–159
Cajan Chicken Hotpot: 174–175

COCKTAILS:

Banana Banshee: 224
Black Russian: 223
Bloody Mary: 227
Blue Lagoon: 220
Brand Alexander: 233
Champagne Cocktail: 212
Grasshopper: 231
Harvey Wallbanger: 216
Mai Tai, 206, 208, 219
Margarita Cocktail: 226
Napoleon's Nightcap: 235
Pina Colada: 214
Tropical Mai Tai: 219

D

Duck:
Crispy Duck Salad: 176–177

Descrts:
Raspberry Cheesecake 239–241
Blueberry Pancakes with Creme Fraise and Raspberries: 242–243
Rhubarb, Raspberry and Pear Crumble: 244–245
Marshmallow Pie: 246–247
Rachael's Chocolate Cake: 252-253

F

Fish and Seafood:
Clam Chowder: 131–133
Manhattan Clam Chowder: 134

Crab Cakes with Spicy Mayo: 142–143

Fillet of Plaice on chunky pea purée with smoked bacon: 188–189
Palm Suite Fish Pie: 190–192
Scottish Mussels in a Whisky Cream & Bacon Sauce: 193–194
Mussels in a Cider and Cream Sauce: 195

H

Hamburgers:
The Bacon and Cheese burger: 97
Blue Stilton and BBQ sauce burger: 98
Rob's Burger: 100
Lamb Burgers with Tomato and Red Pepper Relish: 105
Chicken Burgers topped with Beetroot Relish and Goats Cheese: 107–108
Turkey Burger with a Beetroot & Apple Relish: 109–110

L

Lamb:
Lamb Burger with Tomato and Red Pepper Relish: 105
Rob's Lamb Stew with Spinach and Mint: 157–158
Lamb Meatballs with Roquefort sauce: 170–171
Crispy Lamb Salad with Mint Labneh: 186–187

M

Mushrooms:
Cream of Mushroom Soup: 123
Mushrooms on toast: 138

Meatballs:
Aromatic Beef Meatballs with fresh Tomato Sauce: 166–167
Pork Meatballs: 168–169
Lamb Meatballs with Roquefort sauce: 170–171

O

Onions:
French Onion soup: 125–126

P

Pork:
Pork in Madeira Sauce: 151–152
Pork Belly: 155–156
Pork Meatballs: 168–169
Sweet and Sour Pork: 201

Puddings:
Sticky Toffee Pudding: 237–238
The Queen of Rice Puddings: 248–249
Brioche Bread and Butter Pudding: 250–251

Potatoes:
House fries: 102–103
Cheese & Bacon Skins: 144
Champ: 156

Plantains:
Fried Plantains: 161–162

R

Relish:
Tomato and Red Pepper Relish: 106
Beetroot and Apple Relish: 110

S

Salads:
Thai Poached Chicken Salad with Tahini dressing: 153–154
Crispy Duck Salad: 176–177

Sauces:
Smoky BBQ sauce: 98
Satay sauce: 137
Blue Cheese Dip: 140–141
Spicy Mayo: 142–143
Palm Suite's "Wild West" Steak Sauce: 148–149
Béarnaise Sauce: 150
Madeira Sauce: 151–152
Banana and Papaya Ketchup: 158–159
Tomato Sauce: 163–164
Roquefort Sauce: 170–171
Cream and Brandy Sauce: 178–179

Soups:
Broccoli and Stilton: 120
Cream of Asparagus: 122
Cream of Mushroom: 123
French onion: 125–126
Fresh Tomato: 127–128
Tomato and celery: 129
Clam Chowder: 131–133
Manhattan Clam Chowder: 134

Stocks:
Beef/Veal: 112
Brown Chicken Stock: 113
White Chicken stock: 115
Fish: 116
Vegetable: 117

T

Tomato:
Fresh Tomato soup: 127–128
Tomato and celery soup: 129
Tomato Sauce: 163–164

Turkey:
Turkey Burger with a Beetroot & Apple Relish: 109–110

V

Veal in Bread Crumbs with Capers and Lemon Butter: 202–203
Edna's Vegetarian Nut Bake: 204–205

www.ingramcontent.com/pod-product-compliance
Lightning Source LLC
Chambersburg PA
CBHW042023100526
44587CB00029B/4283